RESEARCH REPORT MARCH 2017

Getting Ready for the Common Core State Standards

Experiences of CPS Teachers and Administrators Preparing for the New Standards

Julia A. Gwynne and Jennifer R. Cowhy

TABLE OF CONTENTS

1 Executive Summary

3 Introduction

Chapter 1
9 Practitioner Beliefs about the Common Core State Standards

Chapter 2
13 Strategies and Supports for Implementing the CCSS

Chapter 3
21 Practitioner Feelings of Preparedness to Teach the CCSS

Chapter 4
25 Schools' Organizational Capacity and Preparation for the CCSS

Chapter 5
31 Interpretive Summary

33 References

35 Appendices

ACKNOWLEDGEMENTS

The authors gratefully acknowledge the many people who contributed to this study. Gudelia Lopez and Peggy Mueller, formerly of the Chicago Community Trust, were early supporters of this work and provided valuable knowledge about how the Chicago Public Schools has worked to support implementation of the Common Core State Standards. Jessica Fulton, Director of Mathematics at CPS, shared important details about her department's work on CCSS implementation. Our colleagues at the UChicago Consortium, including Molly Gordon, Kylie Klein, Holly Hart, and Elaine Allensworth, provided helpful feedback at all stages of this report. In addition, Anna Bruzgulis and Todd Rosenkranz conducted a very thorough technical read of the report, and the UChicago Consortium's communications team, including Bronwyn McDaniel, Jessica Tansey, and Jessica Puller, were instrumental in the production of this brief. We are also grateful to Lynn Cherkasky-Davis for her thoughtful and careful review.

This work was generously funded by the Chicago Community Trust and we thank them for their support. We are also grateful for the operating grants from the Spencer Foundation and the Lewis-Sebring Family Foundation that support the work of the UChicago Consortium.

This report was produced by the UChicago Consortium's publications and communications staff: Bronwyn McDaniel, Director for Outreach and Communication; Jessica Tansey, Communications Manager; and Jessica Puller, Communications Specialist.

Graphic Design: Jeff Hall Design
Photography: Cynthia Howe and David Schalliol
Editing: Jessica Puller and Jessica Tansey

03.2017/pdf/jh.design@rcn.com

Executive Summary

The Common Core State Standards (CCSS) are one of the most significant educational initiatives in the last decade. Aimed at addressing persistently low levels of student achievement in the United States, the CCSS identify the set of skills that students need at each grade level to ensure they are on a path toward college and career readiness.

For many states, including Illinois, the new standards are significantly more rigorous and demanding than the previous standards. This has meant that many teachers must change their instructional practices so that their teaching is aligned with the goals of the new standards. In a large district like the Chicago Public Schools (CPS), which has a workforce of more than 20,000 teachers in over 600 schools, providing professional development on new standards is an enormous endeavor.

The success of any education reform depends on many factors. A critical component is whether school staff are supportive of the initiative and view it as likely to improve educational outcomes. Equally important is whether school staff have the professional development opportunities they need to ensure their practice is aligned with the goals of the initiative. CPS has been preparing to implement the standards since 2011-12. Teachers were expected to teach the new English and Language Arts (ELA) standards by 2013-14 and the new math standards one year later, in 2014-15. This report describes teachers' and administrators' experiences preparing for this transition, using survey responses from the spring of 2014 and the spring of 2015. Survey questions focused on four areas: attitudes about the kind of impact the new standards will have and how challenging they are; experiences with formal professional development on the new standards; opportunities outside of formal training to learn about the new standards; and how prepared teachers feel to teach the new standards.

Key Findings:

- **Elementary teachers were much more optimistic about the impact that the new standards would have on teaching and learning than high school teachers.** Most felt that the CCSS would have a great deal of impact on what they would teach and on how they would teach it. Less than half of high school teachers felt this way.

- **Both elementary and high school teachers felt the impact of the new standards on student achievement would be less than their impact on teaching,** but elementary teachers were still more likely than high school teachers to say that the new standards would have a great deal of impact on achievement.

- **There was wide variation in teachers' reports about the frequency of CCSS-related professional development and, on average, elementary teachers reported participating in more sessions than high school teachers.** Many teachers reported having only 2-4 sessions of professional development in both 2014 and 2015. Moreover, a quarter of high school teachers, and around 15 percent of elementary teachers, reported having no formal professional development on the new standards in either year. For a small group of teachers—just over 20 percent of elementary teachers and around 15 percent of high school teachers—professional development on the new standards occurred more regularly, at least once a month.

- **Many teachers reported frequent interactions with colleagues around the new standards**, even though formal professional development opportunities on the new standards may have been somewhat limited. Two-thirds of elementary teachers and 40 percent of high school teachers reported meeting at least monthly with their colleagues to discuss the standards. Just over half of both groups of teachers reported observing colleagues' classrooms at least once per quarter in an effort to implement the standards.

- **Many teachers reported feeling very prepared on several dimensions related to teaching the standards**, despite the enormous changes that the new standards have brought. Elementary teachers reported feeling more prepared than high school teachers.

    - **In 2014, around half of elementary teachers and 40 percent of high school teachers reported feeling very familiar with the standards and very prepared to teach them.** Fewer than 10 percent of teachers across both grade levels reported feeling unprepared or only a little prepared to teach the standards. Teachers who reported more extensive professional development also reported feeling more prepared to teach the standards.

    - **In 2015, more elementary teachers reported feeling very prepared to teach the standards than in 2014.** Around 60 percent of elementary teachers reported feeling very familiar with and very prepared to teach the new standards. There were also increases in the percent of high school teachers who felt this way, but the increases were not as large as for elementary teachers.

- **Administrators did not report feeling as prepared as teachers in their ability to support implementation of the new standards**, particularly in their ability to evaluate teachers' implementation of the CCSS.

- **Teachers in schools with high levels of organizational capacity reported significantly more extensive standards-related professional development than schools with low levels of organizational capacity.** This was particularly true in schools with high levels of instructional leadership, teacher collaboration, and teacher influence.

- **Teachers in schools with high levels of organizational capacity also reported feeling more prepared to teach the standards, even after taking into account their more extensive professional development.** In other words, regardless of how extensive their standard-related professional development was, teachers who worked in schools with high levels of instructional leadership, teacher collaboration, or teacher influence felt more prepared to teach the new standards.

Many teachers, especially at the elementary level, were optimistic that the new standards would have a great deal of impact on teaching and learning. Despite this, professional development around the new standards has been somewhat limited for many teachers, suggesting that the impact of the Common Core is likely to be uneven, at least initially, across the district. Nevertheless, the district's commitment to a multi-year strategy for preparing teachers to teach the new standards is noteworthy, as is the increase between 2014 and 2015 in how prepared teachers felt to teach the standards. Of course, changing teacher practice is not easy, and ongoing support of teachers is likely to play a critical role in ensuring that teachers' increased familiarity and comfort with the standards ultimately translates into improved teaching and learning. High school staff, in particular, may need ongoing support as they work to increase their familiarity and comfort with the new standards. Administrators may also need more targeted support so that they feel better prepared to provide useful feedback to teachers on their instruction and whether it is aligned with the goals and content of the new standards.

Introduction

Adoption of the Common Core State Standards (CCSS) represents one of the most significant educational initiatives in the last decade. Developed in response to concerns that U.S. students lag behind other countries in their academic achievement and also that achievement gaps between groups of students in this country continue to persist, the CCSS outline a set of national standards intended to increase the level of academic rigor for all students in kindergarten through twelfth grade. The standards aim to accomplish this by placing a great emphasis on higher-order thinking skills rather than rote memorization; they also privilege depth over breadth in the topics covered at each grade level.[1]

Illinois is one of many states for which the new standards represent a significant shift toward more focus on rigorous content and skill development.[2] Many districts within the state, including Chicago Public Schools (CPS), are finding that they need to overhaul their curriculum and provide support to their teachers as they work to implement the new standards. Teachers may not only need to deepen their content knowledge in a subject area, but they may also need to adopt new instructional practices so that their teaching is more closely aligned with the goals of the CCSS. Yet, even with the strongest of supports and the most carefully crafted plan, it is difficult for educators—at all levels of the system—to change practice.[3]

The CCSS are most likely to influence instructional practices when they are strategically aligned with not only strong supports, including curriculum and professional development, but also accountability systems, such as assessments and teacher evaluation systems.[4] Without the incorporation of accountability and a high-alignment environment, teachers may be left to make sense of the reform on their own, drawing upon their own knowledge and often resulting in only surface-level changes. In this case, the new standards could meet the same fate of so many other policies intended to improve instruction in classrooms but failing to bring about real change. Preliminary research on Common Core implementation supports these claims. For example, research has shown that teachers who reported more frequent professional development around the new standards and teachers who received more frequent feedback from classroom observations had students who made greater gains on the math portion of the new Common Core-aligned assessment.[5]

This study examines CPS teachers' and administrators' experiences preparing to teach the new ELA and math standards and is the first in a series of reports that examines implementation of the CCSS in CPS. Subsequent studies will focus on students' instructional experiences and how learning outcomes have changed since the implementation of the new standards.

---

1 Achieve, The Education Trust, & Thomas B. Fordham Foundation (2004); ACT, Inc. (2012); Conley (2014); Common Core Standards Initiative (2014).
2 Carmichael, Martino, Porter-Magee, & Wilson (2010).
3 Dembo & Gibson (1985); Mumtaz (2000); Hargreaves (2005).
4 Coburn, Hill, & Spillane (2016).
5 Kane, Owens, Marinell, Thal, & Staiger (2016).

The Origins of the Common Core State Standards

Standards have been a component of educational policy and practice since 1994, when the reauthorization of the Elementary and Secondary Education Act (ESEA) required states to establish rigorous content standards for all students. The hope was that setting guidelines about what teachers should be teaching would lead to substantially better student outcomes. Yet, not much changed in response to this new school-based accountability. In 2001, No Child Left Behind (NCLB) deepened the national standards-based commitment by adding standardized test scores to school-based accountability, which necessitated a disaggregation of test-score data by student group. While NCLB served to highlight achievement gaps within and between states, it also revealed enormous variation between states in the rigor of their content-standards, the criteria for "proficiency," and even the degree to which state accountability tests matched state content standards. In the wake of NCLB, there were growing concerns that state standards were not adequately preparing students for success in college or the workforce and that U.S. students persistently lagged behind their international peers.[A]

In response to these concerns, the National Governor's Association for Best Practices (NGA) and the Council of Chief State School Officers (CCSSO) came together to create a set of rigorous standards for students in kindergarten through twelfth grade in math and ELA. The standards do not dictate how they should be taught, but instead provide clear expectations for what students should be mastering, naming both skills and content that are important within each grade level. Some skills are emphasized and interwoven through all grade-level standards in both subjects; these are the skills that research and international benchmarks have named as important to success in college and the workforce, including collaboration, communication, critical-thinking, and problem-solving skills.[B]

Both sets of standards are a major departure from most states' previous standards. The ELA standards across all grade levels have shifted in three overarching ways: they call for students to 1) regularly engage in complex texts; 2) practice grounding their reading, writing, and speaking in informational and literary texts; and 3) build knowledge through nonfictional texts rich in content matter. While ELA teachers are predominantly responsible for implementing the ELA standards, other teachers and subjects (i.e., history and science) are also expected to engage students with complex texts outside of literature. There are also three key shifts in the math standards, which call for: 1) a greater focus on fewer topics, addressing the "mile wide and inch-deep" phenomenon often characterizing math instruction; 2) topics building on each other, creating greater coherence across the standards; and 3) more rigor and a focus on developing conceptual understanding and applications to real life, as well as developing procedural skills and fluency.[C]

A National Academy of Education (2009).
B Common Core State Standards Initiative (2014).
C Common Core State Standards Initiative (2014).

CPS Strategy for Supporting Professional Learning on CCSS

After Illinois adopted the CCSS in 2010, CPS recognized that it would need ample time to prepare its teachers to teach the new standards. The district began developing a multi-year strategy in 2011-12 for preparing its workforce, with professional development for staff beginning in 2012-13 and continuing through 2015-16. Teachers were expected to teach the new ELA standards by 2013-14 and the new math standards one year later, in 2014-15. In the 2015-16 school year, the district began developing the next phase of professional learning to support its teachers.

The district chose an approach somewhat similar to a "train the trainer" model for providing professional development around the new standards. This approach leveraged the fact that all schools in CPS are organized into networks, which provide a range of support services and also serve as a central hub for information about policies and practices in the district. Networks identified a small group of experienced teachers (teacher facilitators) from their schools to participate in three to four cycles of district-sponsored professional development during each school year. Teacher facilitators then shared their experiences at Teacher Leader Institutes with a group of teacher leaders sent by each school within their network. In turn, these teacher leaders were expected to share their professional development experiences and learning with colleagues in their own schools.[6]

The district used different strategies for developing the content of its ELA and math professional learning experiences. The Department of Literacy selected a number of "early adopter" schools to assist them in developing the professional development activities. Schools had to apply for early adopter status and, as a part of the application process, they had to demonstrate that they were already using instructional approaches aligned with the new standards. Professional support for the new ELA standards was launched during the 2012-13 school year and was differentiated by grade levels (K-2 and 3-12). Participation was optional during this first year, although most networks chose to participate. Beginning in 2013-14, the first year of full implementation for the ELA standards, participation in professional development was mandatory for all networks. As of 2015-16, networks could choose whether to participate in district-sponsored professional development or provide their own professional learning opportunities (**see Figure 1** for timeline).[7]

The early adopter schools also developed assessment and instructional activities aligned to the new ELA standards. Grade-level teams at each early adopter school spent the 2012-13 school year developing curricular units, which included a curriculum map, a unit plan, and corresponding texts to be used in the classroom. Once the units were developed, they were made available to all schools in the district through an online

FIGURE 1
CPS Implementation Timeline for the Common Core State Standards

	Common Core State Standards Implementation	Other District Changes
2011-2012	District announces a three-year transition plan to train teachers on Common Core State Standards. Schools apply and district identifies early adopter schools responsible for assisting in the design of ELA professional development, assessments and instructional materials.	District announces plan to implement an extended school day the following school year. CPS-CTU Joint Teacher Committe begins to design and plan for implementation of new evaluation system, Recognizing Educators Advancing Chicago Students (REACH).
2012-2013	Department of Literacy launches professional development for ELA teachers. Participation optional for networks. Department of Mathematics launches professional development for teachers in grades six through twelve. Participation optional for networks.	District implements an extended school day. CPS begins implementing REACH in all schools for non-tenured teachers only.
2013-2014	K-12 teachers begin teaching ELA standards. Math professional development mandatory for K-12 teachers.	Implementation of REACH begins for all (tenured and non-tenured) teachers.
2014-2015	K-12 teachers begin teaching math standards. Schools are able to purchase CCSS-aligned instructional materials from district-approved list.	
2015-2016	Math and ELA professional development becomes optional for all networks.	

---

6 Chicago Public Schools (n.d.); CPS staff, personal communication (December 15, 2015).

7 Chicago Public Schools (2015).

resource center. The district hoped that their strategy of using an online resource center would allow teachers across the district to engage with the new standards, reflect on their own practice, and learn from colleagues as everyone worked to create new and deeper learning opportunities for their students.[8]

The Department of Mathematics opted for a different strategy to support professional learning around the new standards for its teachers. It partnered with staff from two local universities, DePaul University and the Erikson Institute, and from its inception, professional development focused on *how* to teach high-quality math, rather than a more narrow focus on *what* skills are required by the new standards at each grade level. Training began in 2012-13 for teachers in grades 6-12. Although professional development was optional during this first year, most networks chose to participate. In 2013-14, participation in professional development was mandatory for all networks and was differentiated by grade level (pre-kindergarten-5 and 6-12).[9] Beginning in 2015-16, the district returned to an opt-in model for networks, allowing them to choose their own form of professional development; however, most networks have continued to participate in district-sponsored professional development.[10]

Four networks received additional intensive support in their math-related professional learning from DePaul and Erikson. Two of these networks had preexisting partnerships with DePaul supporting their math instruction. The other two were chosen by the district, based on having a high-needs student population and their demonstrated support of the Network Partnership model. The intensive support provided by these two partners included the creation of professional learning communities, which extended and deepened the learning from the Teacher Leader Institutes. Additionally, university staff provided individual and collaborative coaching to small group of teachers within these networks.[11]

District Challenges with CCSS Implementation

As the district launched its standards-related professional development, a number of questions and concerns emerged, particularly among high school staff. Many high schools in CPS, especially those with a college-preparatory focus, had relied on the ACT College and Career Readiness Standards to guide instruction for a number of years. These standards had the benefit of having a strong instructional focus and were aligned with the standardized tests in use at the high school level. The introduction of the CCSS generated some confusion about which standards high school teachers should use, and many schools were reluctant to abandon the College and Career Readiness Standards, which they felt had been effective for preparing students for college.

High school staff were also concerned by the district's decision to transition all grades to the new standards in a single year (2013-14 for the ELA standards and 2014-15 for the math standards). Many felt that lack of a phased-in approach put high school students and teachers at a great disadvantage. Given that the standards at each grade level build on standards in earlier grade levels, high school students were expected to learn more challenging content without the benefit of exposure to the standards in earlier grades.[12] Compounding these issues for high school staff was the fact that schools were reorganized into a different network structure in November 2013. High schools went from having their own network structure to being included in networks with elementary schools. Since most of the teachers within each new network were now elementary teachers, many high school teachers felt that the distinctive needs of high schools, particularly around Common Core implementation, were not addressed in the new network structure.

Another issue that affected both elementary and high schools in their efforts to implement the new standards

---

8 Chicago Public Schools (2015); Former CPS staff, personal communication (June 23, 2016).
9 Although the CCSS does not include standards for preschool-aged students, the Department of Mathematics included preschool teachers in their professional development.
10 CPS staff, personal communication (December 15, 2016).
11 Foundation staff, personal communication (July 12, 2016); University staff, personal communication (July 15, 2016).
12 This was also a stated concern of many elementary teachers.

was the near-simultaneous launch of the new teacher evaluation system. Many teachers felt the two initiatives were not well integrated and they were confused about how to reconcile what felt like two distinctly different frameworks for teaching. The district has worked to resolve this conflict by emphasizing that the new standards provide a framework for what teachers should teach while the new teacher evaluation systems offers a framework for how teachers should teach.

Finally, another complication resulted from the district's decision to delay purchasing new instructional materials until the spring of 2015. The decision was made with the hope of preventing schools from wasting limited resources on materials that weren't really aligned with the Common Core. The district needed time to thoroughly vet materials, but delaying all purchasing until the spring of 2015 meant that teachers had to supply their own materials or make use of resources available on the CPS online resource center during the first 1-2 years of implementation.[13]

Teachers' and Administrators' Experiences with CCSS

Although the district has been providing professional development on the new standards for several years, relatively little is known about how successful these efforts have been in making sure that all teachers are receiving the high-quality professional development they need to teach the new standards. This report uses survey responses to examine CPS teachers' and administrators' experiences with the CCSS. Each year, the University of Chicago Consortium on School Research (UChicago Consortium) administers a districtwide survey, *My Voice, My School*, to all teachers in CPS. In 2014 and 2015, the annual teacher survey included a series of questions about the CCSS, which were asked of teachers who either taught in self-contained classrooms or were subject-specific teachers.[14] Among respondents who indicated that they taught a specific subject, only those whose primary subject was ELA or math were included in the analyses. (**See Appendix A** for additional details about the sample.) In 2014 and 2015, the UChicago Consortium also administered surveys to principals and assistant principals. An initial analysis revealed few differences between principals and assistant principals, so their responses have been combined. Teacher and administrator responses are presented based on the survey year and also grade level (elementary vs. high school). We also examine whether there were differences across schools and networks in teachers' professional development experiences and in how prepared they feel to teach the standards.

This report is organized in the following way:

Chapter 1 examines teachers' and administrators' attitudes about the impact they feel the CCSS will have on teaching and learning and how challenging they believe the new standards will be for their students.

Chapter 2 explores school staff's experiences with CCSS-related professional development and other strategies for successful implementation of the standards. It also examines barriers that school staff have experienced in their efforts to implement the new standards.

Chapter 3 describes how prepared teachers feel to teach the standards.

Chapter 4 examines how schools' organizational capacity is related to the professional development that teachers received and to how prepared they felt to teach the standards.

Chapter 5 summarizes key findings and discusses implications of this research.

---

13 Former CPS staff member, personal communication (April 5, 2016).
14 Unfortunately, the survey did not ask separate questions about ELA standards training and math standards training.

CHAPTER 1

Practitioner Beliefs about the Common Core State Standards

The success of any education reform depends in part on how those who are responsible for implementing the reform react to and make sense of it.[15] In the case of Common Core, whether teachers enact practices that are consistent with the standards depends on their interpretation and understanding of what the new standards mean for their own practice and for student achievement. Particularly important is whether teachers view Common Core as appropriate, reasonable, and likely to be effective in achieving its goal of improving student achievement.[16] In a district that serves many students with distinctive educational needs, including students with academic skills far below grade level, students with disabilities, and English Language Learners (ELL), teachers may have real concerns about how appropriate the new standards will be for their students. Research has shown that implementation is often more restricted among teachers who view reforms as unlikely to be effective.[17]

This chapter examines teachers' and administrators' attitudes about the new standards in 2014 and 2015. We find that most elementary teachers and administrators believed that the CCSS would have a great deal of impact on teaching; however, high school teachers and administrators were much less likely to feel this way. Teachers and administrators, regardless of their grade level, felt the impact of the new standards on student achievement was likely to be less than the impact on teaching. Close to half of all teachers also viewed the new standards as very challenging for their students.

CCSS Impact on Teaching and Learning

Elementary teachers were much more optimistic about the impact the new standards would have on teaching and learning than high school teachers. Around three-quarters of elementary teachers in both 2014 and 2015 felt that the CCSS would have a great deal of impact on *what* teachers teach, and two-thirds felt that the CCSS would have a great deal of impact on *how* teachers teach. Less than half of high school teachers felt this way (**see Figure 2**).[18]

Both elementary and high school teachers felt the impact of CCSS on student achievement would be less than their impact on teaching, but elementary teachers were still more likely than high school teachers to say that the new standards would have a great deal of impact on achievement.[19]

High school teachers' ambivalence about the impact of the new standards may be a reflection of their concerns about whether and how to implement them. As described in the Introduction, many high school teachers were reluctant to switch to the new standards after having used the ACT College and Career Readiness standards for a number of years. In addition, high school teachers felt the lack of a phased transition put their students at great disadvantage.

---

15 Coburn et al. (2016); Honig (2006); Datnow & Castellano (2000); Louis, Febey, & Shroeder (2005); Gold (2002); Louis & Dentler (1988).
16 Witt & Elliott (1985); Donnell & Gettinger (2015).
17 Witt & Elliott (1985).
18 Elementary and high school teachers had statistically different responses on each survey item included in this report. Elementary and high school administrators had statistically different responses on most survey items, but not all. See Appendix A for additional details.
19 Administrator reports about the impact that the CCSS would have were very similar to teacher reports, with elementary administrators more likely to say the new standards would have a great deal of impact than high school administrators. See Figure B.1 in Appendix B for details.

FIGURE 2

Elementary Teachers Were More Likely than High School Teachers to Say that the CCSS Would Have a Great Deal of Impact on Teaching and Learning

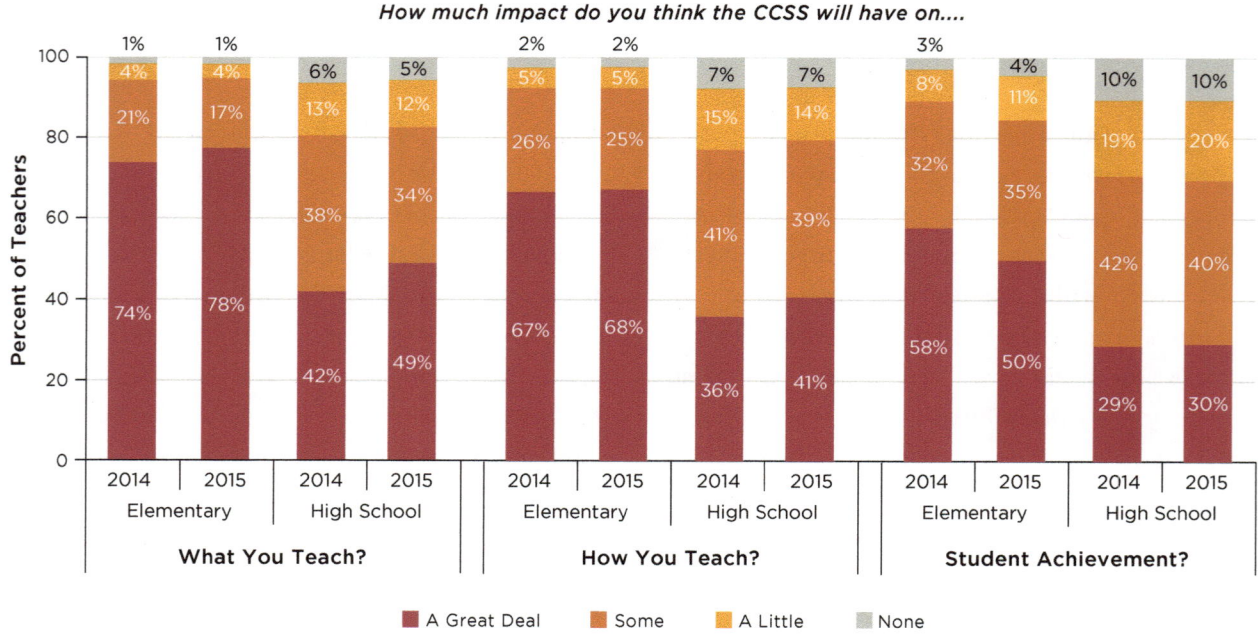

Note: Percentages may not add up to 100 due to rounding.

Challenging Standards for Students

Perhaps one reason why practitioners felt the new standards would have less of an impact on student achievement than on teaching was because most viewed them as being very challenging for their students. Challenging coursework can lead to students disengaging from the learning process, thereby minimizing the potential for positive impact of the new standards.[20]

Around half of all teachers said that the standards are very challenging and another 40 percent or so say the standards are somewhat challenging (**see Figure 3**).[21] However, the proportion of teachers who said the standards are very challenging did not vary much depending on the characteristics of the students in the schools where they teach. Teachers who worked in schools serving high proportions of low-achieving students, students with disabilities, or ELL students were somewhat more likely to view the standards as very challenging for their students than teachers who were in schools where the proportions of these students is low, but the difference is fewer than 10 percentage points (**see Figure 4**). In other words, many teachers viewed the standards as very challenging regardless of the students they teach.

---

20 Allensworth, Gwynne, Pareja, Sebastian & Stevens (2014).
21 Slightly higher percentages of elementary and high school administrators (60 percent and 56 percent, respectively) felt the new standards are very challenging for students. See Figure B.2 in Appendix B.

Chapter 1 | Practitioner Beliefs about the Common Core State Standards

FIGURE 3

Close to Half of All Teachers Thought the CCSS Would Be Very Challenging for Their Students

How challenging do you think the CCSS are for your students?

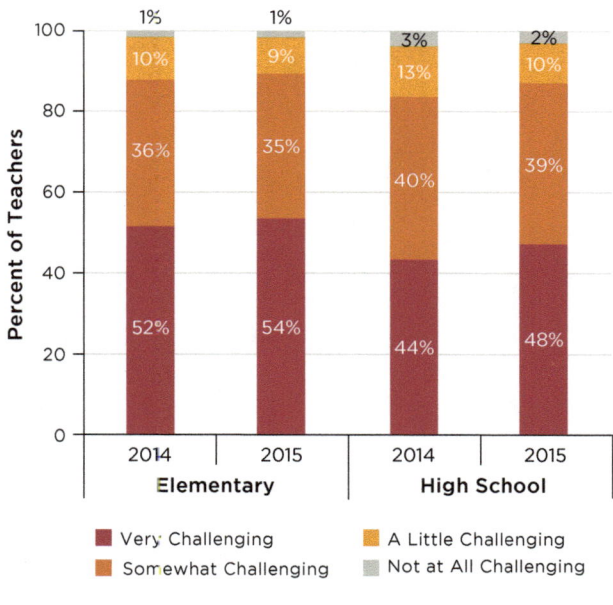

- Very Challenging
- Somewhat Challenging
- A Little Challenging
- Not at All Challenging

Note: Percentages may not add up to 100 due to rounding.

FIGURE 4

Teachers' Perceptions of How Challenging CCSS Will Be for Students Shows Little Variation by Their Schools' Student Composition

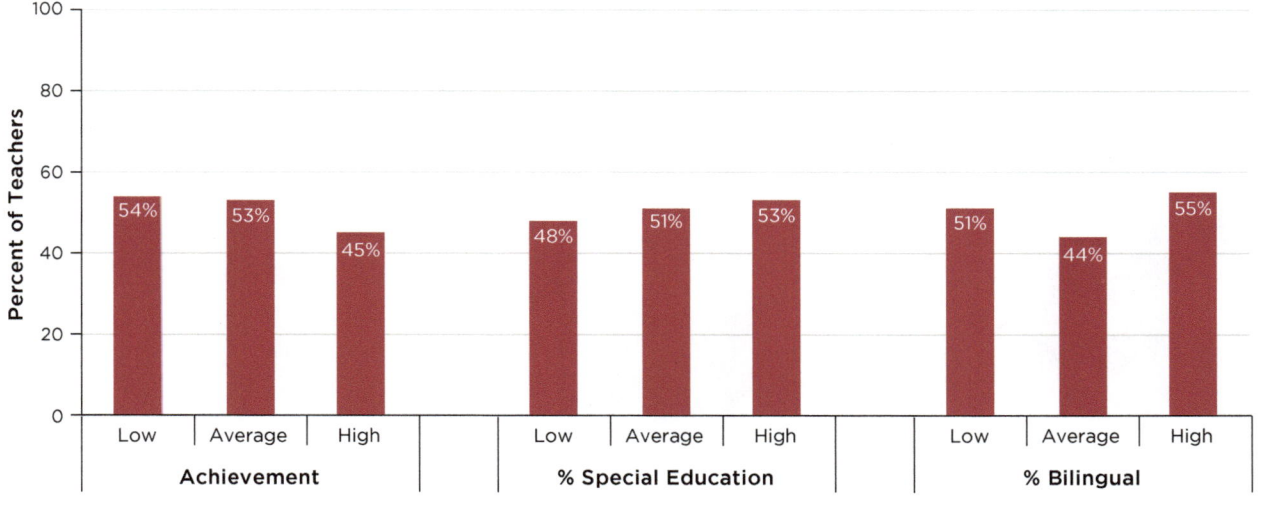

Note: Schools were ranked into three equal-sized groups for each compositional measure included in Figure 4.

CHAPTER 2

Strategies and Supports for Implementing the CCSS

Ensuring that teachers and administrators have adequate support in their efforts to implement the CCSS is critical if the new standards are to result in improved learning outcomes for students. Teachers must not only learn the content of the new standards and how they differ from the old standards, but they may also need help identifying best practices for teaching the new standards, particularly for different populations of students. Administrators may need to learn how to provide constructive feedback to teachers as they grapple with incorporating the new standards into their instructional practices.

The traditional forum for providing professional development to school staff, the one-day workshop, can be useful for explaining new initiatives or providing an overview of new teaching strategies, but it's not always effective for changing practice.[22] Teacher practice and student achievement are most likely to change when teachers experience sustained and ongoing professional development and when they have opportunities to practice new approaches and receive feedback on their efforts. Coaching can be particularly effective in helping teachers implement new instructional practices, since it identifies areas where teachers are successfully implementing a new strategy as well as areas where more work is needed.[23] Research has shown that teachers may need at least 50 hours of instruction, practice, and coaching to achieve mastery of a new skill.[24]

Ensuring that teachers have opportunities to collaborate with colleagues can also play an important role in helping teachers change practice.[25] Regular collaboration allows teachers to exchange ideas about best practices for teaching the new standards and helps them to coordinate teaching within and across grade levels. But frequent collaboration requires a significant time commitment, and competing demands on teachers' time may hinder these efforts.

This chapter explores teachers' and administrators' reports about CCSS-related professional development and the kinds of topics covered in sessions. It also looks at teachers' opportunities to collaborate with colleagues around the new standards, and whether other activities beyond professional development and collaboration occurred to promote successful implementation of the standards. Finally, it identifies barriers that school staff experienced in their efforts to incorporate the new standards.

Formal Professional Development on CCSS

There was wide variation in teachers' reports about the frequency of formal professional development on the new standards. Many teachers reported participating in only 1-2 sessions each semester or 2-4 sessions per year, which likely falls short of the 50 hours of professional development that research suggests teachers need. Moreover, a quarter of high school teachers and nearly 15 percent of elementary teachers reported that they had no professional development around the new standards in either year. A small group of teachers reported very extensive standards-related professional development. Around 20 percent of elementary teachers and 15 percent of high school teachers reported attending professional development around the new standards at least monthly (see Figure 5).

Administrators' reports of CCSS-related professional development were somewhat similar to those of their teachers, with elementary administrators reporting more frequent professional development than their high school colleagues. Like teachers, the most typical experience was 1-2 sessions per semester (see Figure 6). However, one-fifth of high school administrators reported no professional development in 2014, compared to 7 percent of elementary administrators.

---

22 Darling-Hammond, Chung Wei, Andree, & Richardson (2009).
23 Truesdale (2003).
24 Gulamhussein (2013); French (1997).
25 Bryk, Sebring, Allensworth, Luppescu, & Easton (2010).

FIGURE 5

Around 40 Percent of Elementary Teachers and Half of High School Teachers Reported Receiving Professional Development at most Once a Year

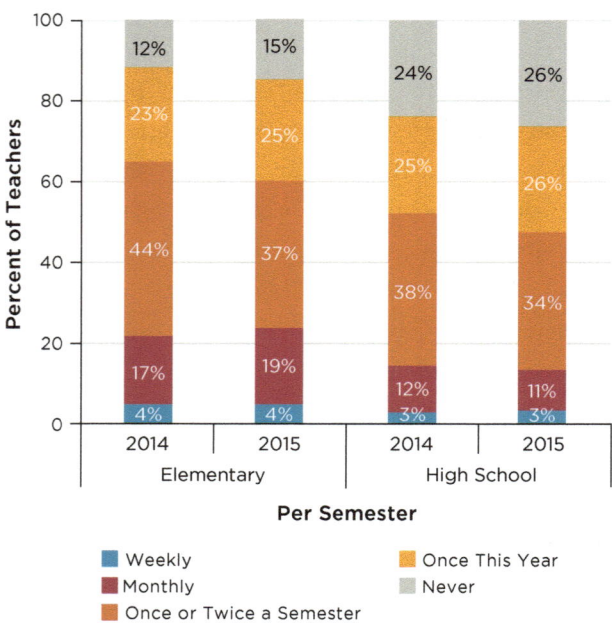

FIGURE 6

Around a Third of Elementary Administrators and Half of High School Administrators Reported Receiving Professional Development at most Once a Year in 2014

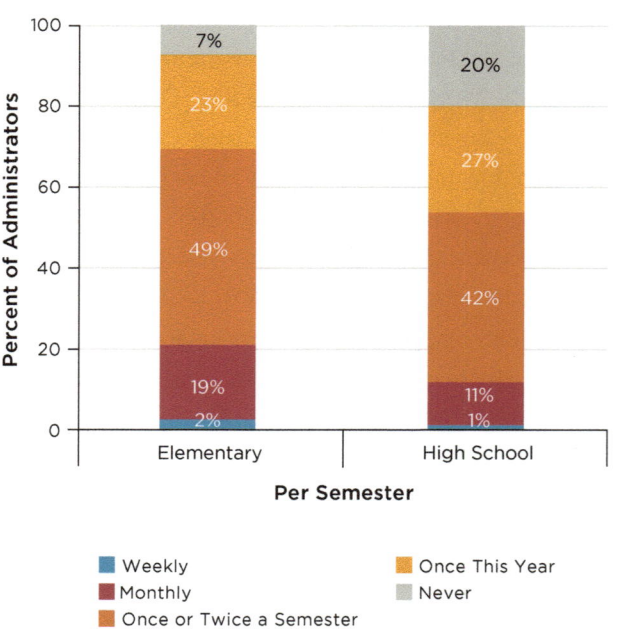

Note: Percentages may not add up to 100 due to rounding.

Note: This item comes from the 2014 Administrator Survey. Percentages may not add up to 100 due to rounding.

Topics Covered During Professional Development

More than three-quarters of elementary teachers in 2014 and 2015 reported that the new math and ELA standards were covered in their professional development sessions (**see Figure 7**). But only 55 to 60 percent of elementary teachers in each year reported topics such as curriculum materials and resources, adaptation of classroom assessments, research on best practices and the new standardized assessments (i.e., PARCC) were included. Even fewer teachers, around 40 percent, reported that strategies for teaching the new standards to subgroups of students were included.

Professional development for high school teachers was less comprehensive than for elementary teachers in both 2014 and 2015. Only two-thirds to three-quarters of high school teachers reported that math and ELA standards were included in their professional development sessions, and fewer than half reported that topics such as curriculum materials, adaptation of classroom assessments, and the new standardized assessments were included. Finally, only 30 percent reported that their professional learning covered teaching the new standards to specific subgroups of students. There were few differences between 2014 and 2015 in teachers' reports about which topics were covered in professional development sessions (**see Figure 7**).

Chapter 2 | Strategies and Supports for Implementing the CCSS

FIGURE 7
Most Teachers Reported that Math and ELA Standards have been Covered in their Professional Development but Many Fewer Teachers Reported Other Topics Were Covered

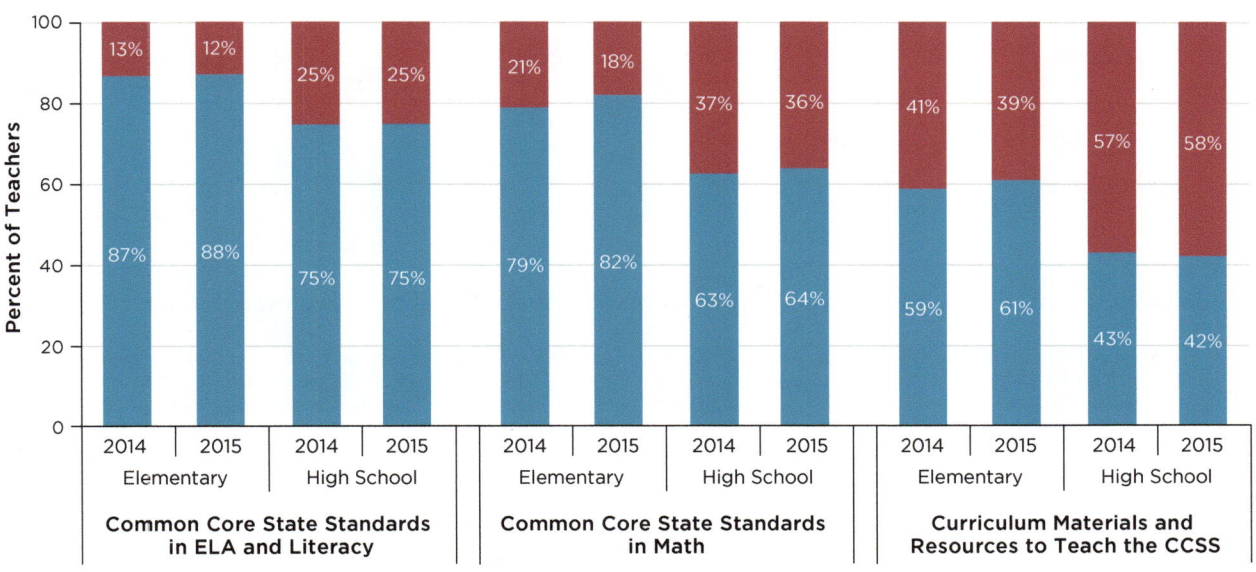

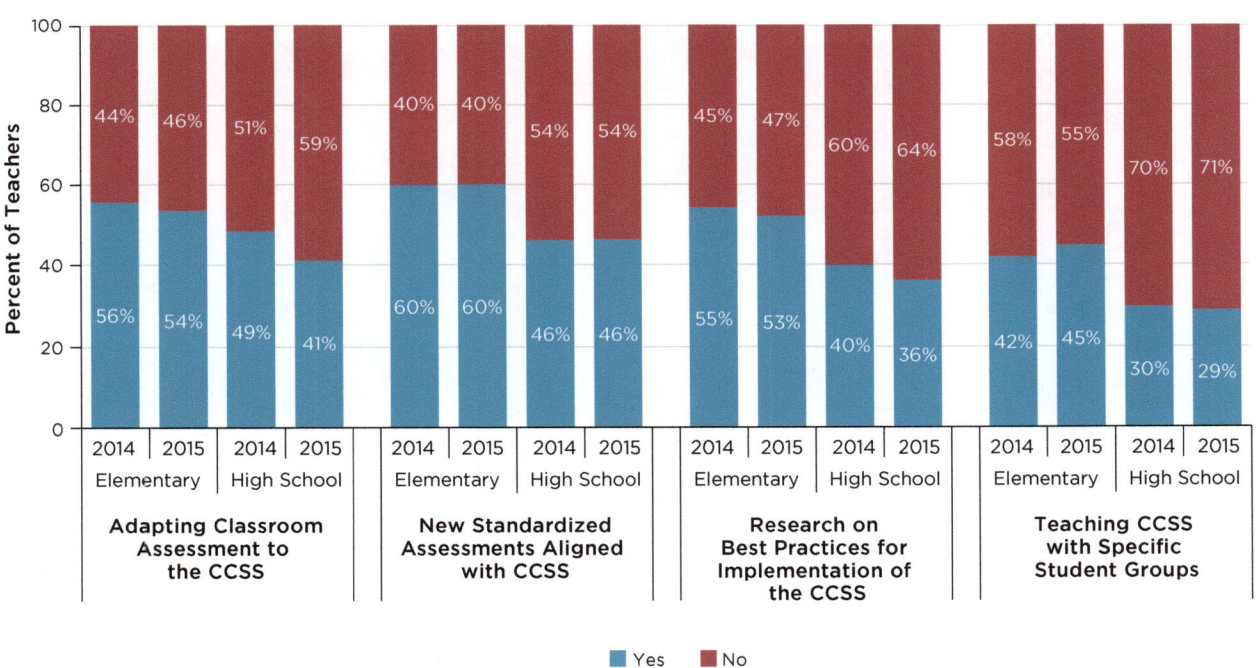

Note: Percentages may not add up to 100 due to rounding.

What Was the Quality of Standards-Related Professional Development?

While the frequency of standards-related professional development sessions and the coverage of topics during these sessions are important components of preparing teachers to teach the new standards, equally important is whether sessions are of high quality. The 2014 and 2015 *My Voice, My School* surveys did not ask teachers to rate the quality of their CCSS-related training directly; however, teachers were asked to describe their overall professional development experiences during each year. Figure A shows that teachers who reported very extensive standards-related professional development in 2014 were four times more likely to strongly agree that their professional development had been sustained and focused than teachers whose standards related professional development was not very extensive. They were also four times more likely to strongly agree that it had included enough time to think carefully about, try, and evaluate new ideas.

FIGURE A

Quality of Overall Professional Development, by Extensiveness of CCSS-Related Professional Development

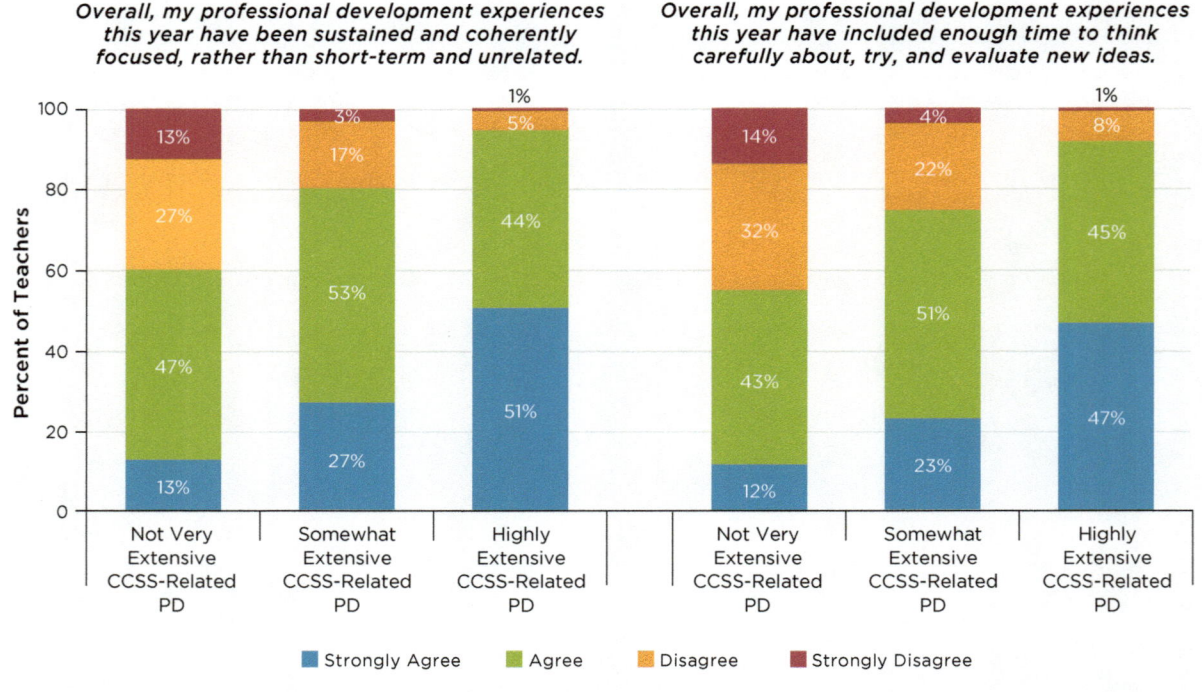

Note: Responses come from the 2014 *My Voice, My School* teacher survey. Extensiveness of standards-related professional development is measured by combining the teachers responses about the frequency of professional development with the topics covered. See Appendix A for additional details on how the extensiveness of professional development is measured and how the categories in this figure are determined. Percentages may not add up to 100 due to rounding.

Collaboration with Colleagues Around CCSS

Although formal professional development around the CCSS may have been limited for some teachers, many, especially at the elementary level, reported frequent meetings with colleagues outside of formal learning opportunities to talk about the new standards. Around 40 percent of elementary teachers said they met weekly with colleagues to discuss the CCSS, while another quarter reported meeting monthly. This kind of informal collaboration around the standards was less frequent at the high school level, with just over 20 percent of teachers saying they met with colleagues weekly and another 20 percent saying they met monthly (**see Figure 8**).

Administrators were somewhat more optimistic about the frequency that teachers met to talk about the standards, with over half of elementary and high school administrators saying teachers met in teams across grade levels at least weekly. Many administrators also reported that teachers regularly observed each other's classroom to help implement the CCSS, although this happened far less frequently than meeting in grade-level teams to discuss the new standards (see Figure 9).

Administrator Supports for CCSS Implementation

Administrators also worked to support implementation of the standards in their schools. Around 85 percent of elementary administrators and 75 percent of high school administrators reported that they sent school staff to professional development, adjusted their school improvement plans to accommodate standards-related activities, created a leadership plan for implementing the new standards, and modified students assessments to include CCSS-related activities (see Figure 10). Slightly lower proportions, but still more than half of all administrators, said that they had modified math and ELA curriculum to align with the new standards and convened departmental groups to learn about CCSS. One area where administrators were less likely to report activity was purchasing curriculum materials aligned with the new standards: only half of all elementary administrators and a third of high school administrators reported doing so by 2014. The lack of schoolwide purchasing of these materials in over half of all schools meant that teachers had to spend time finding instructional resources that they could use to supplement their teaching.

Barriers to CCSS Implementation

Administrators identified a number of barriers to implementing the new standards. One concern that both elementary and high school administrators shared was being held accountable for tests that are not aligned to the new standards.[26] Elementary administrators also felt that insufficient time for teachers to collaborate was an issue. Few administrators felt that lack of math content knowledge or inadequate professional development were particularly problematic issues (see Figure 11).

FIGURE 8
Significantly More Elementary Teachers than High School Teachers Reported Meeting at least Monthly with their Colleagues to Talk about the CCSS Outside of Professional Development

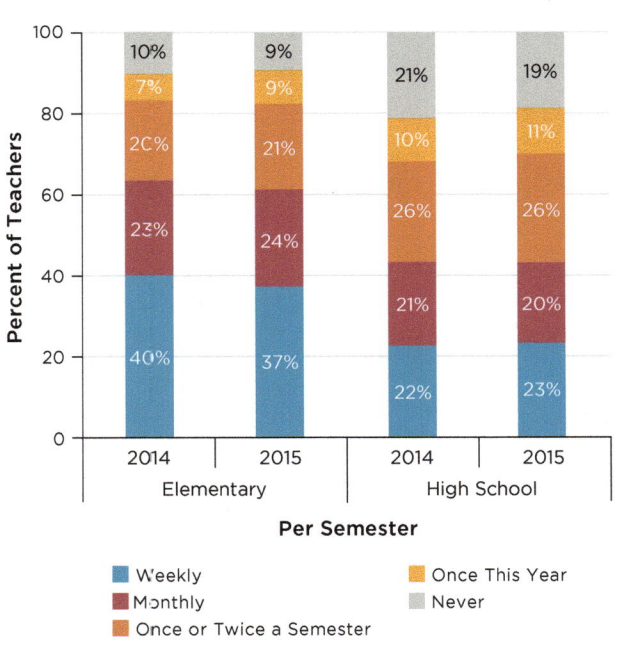

Outside of professional development, how often have you met with other teachers to discuss the CCSS so far this year?

Note: Percentages may not add up to 100 due to rounding.

FIGURE 9
Many Administrators Reported Teachers Observed One Another at least Quarterly to Help Implement the CCSS

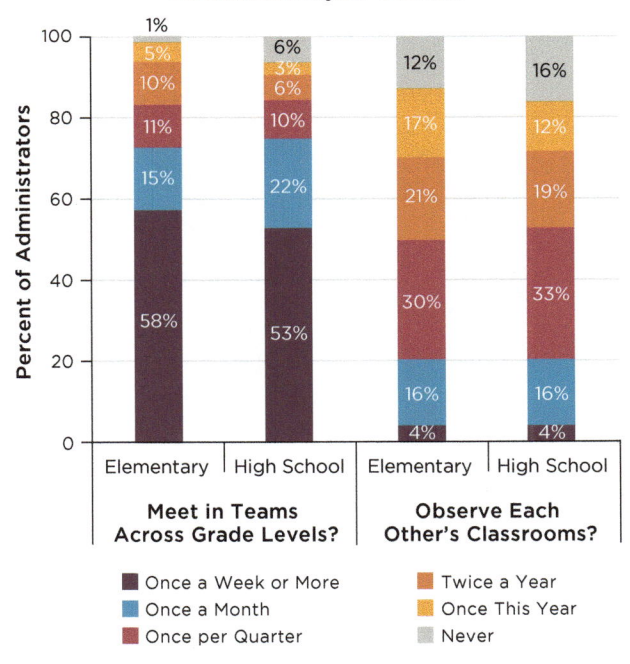

To help implement the CCSS, how often do teachers in your school...

Note: This item was only included on the 2015 Administrator Survey.

26 Elementary schools are required to administer the NWEA MAP test for accountability purposes.

FIGURE 10

Administrators, Especially Elementary Administrators, Were More Likely Than Not to Say They Had Taken the Following Steps to Implement the CCSS

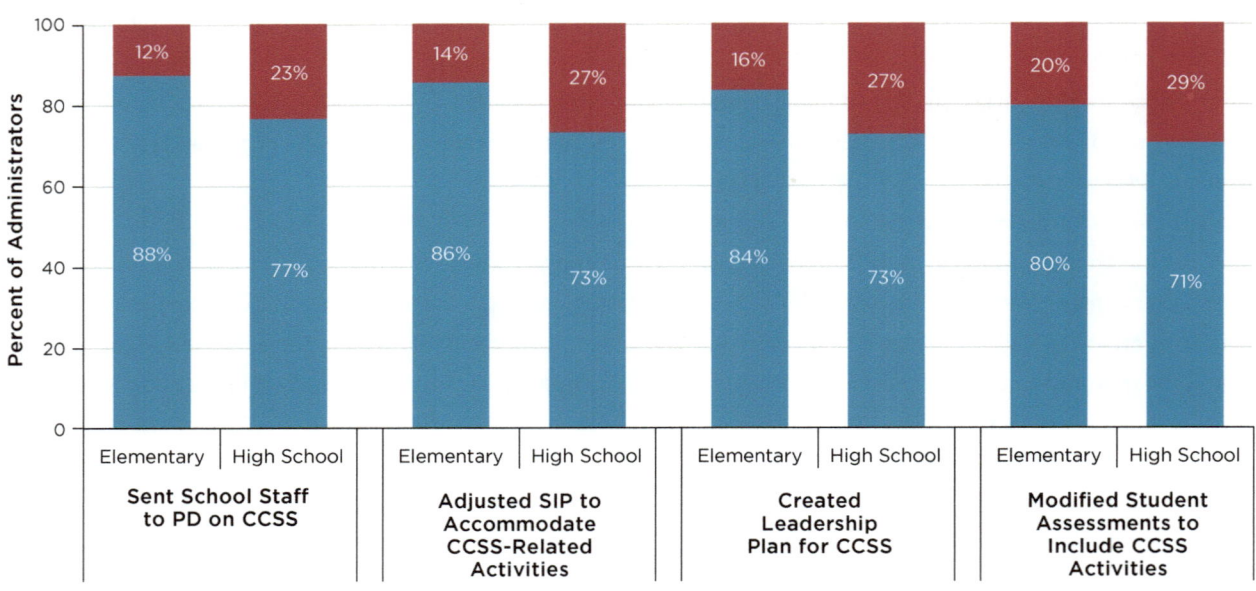

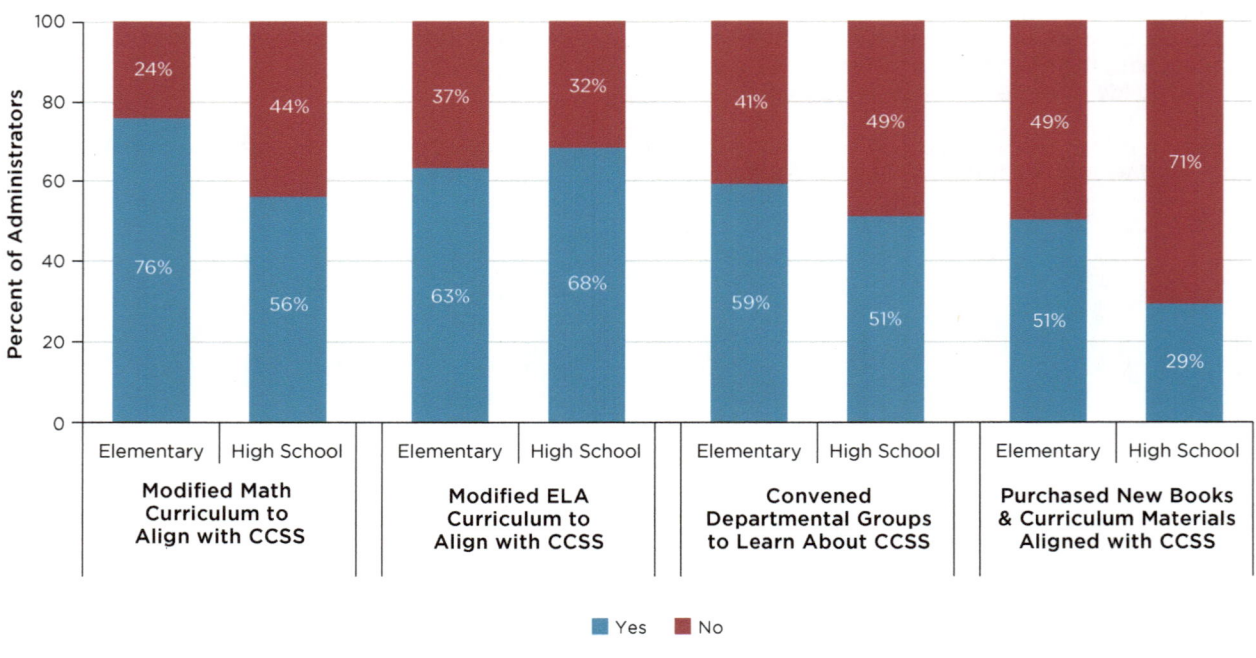

Note: These items were only included on the 2014 Administrator Survey.

FIGURE 11

Nearly Half of All Administrators Reported that Being Held Accountable for Student Assessments not Aligned with the CCSS was a Barrier to CCSS Implementation

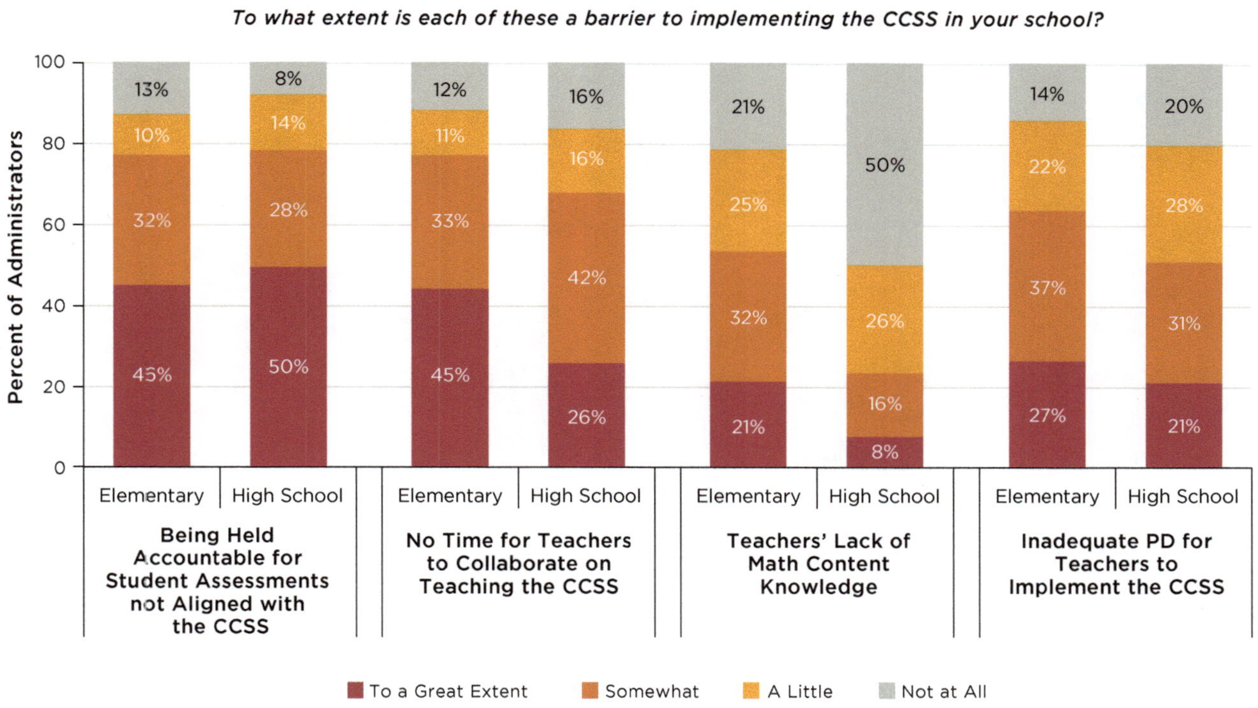

To what extent is each of these a barrier to implementing the CCSS in your school?

Barrier	Level	Elementary	High School
Being Held Accountable for Student Assessments not Aligned with the CCSS	To a Great Extent	45%	50%
	Somewhat	32%	28%
	A Little	10%	14%
	Not at All	13%	8%
No Time for Teachers to Collaborate on Teaching the CCSS	To a Great Extent	45%	26%
	Somewhat	33%	42%
	A Little	11%	16%
	Not at All	12%	16%
Teachers' Lack of Math Content Knowledge	To a Great Extent	21%	8%
	Somewhat	32%	16%
	A Little	25%	26%
	Not at All	21%	50%
Inadequate PD for Teachers to Implement the CCSS	To a Great Extent	27%	21%
	Somewhat	37%	31%
	A Little	22%	28%
	Not at All	14%	20%

Note: These items were only included on the 2015 Administrator Survey. Percentages may not add up to 100 due to rounding.

CHAPTER 3

Practitioner Feelings of Preparedness to Teach the CCSS

Teachers' beliefs about their ability to achieve instructional outcomes in the classroom can be an important indicator of how successful they are in actually accomplishing them.[27] Prior research has found that teachers' self-efficacy is not only related to the effort that they put into their instruction but it is also related to their willingness to change their practice and to try new things to better serve their students.[28] A strong sense of self-efficacy among teachers has been shown to positively affect student motivation and also student achievement.[29]

In the case of Common Core, teachers' beliefs about how prepared they feel to teach the new standards can be an indication of how successful they are in teaching them and how likely it is that student achievement will improve as a result. This chapter examines teachers' feelings of preparedness on a range of topics related to implementing the standards: knowledge about the standards, feeling prepared to teach them, having sufficient materials for teaching, and having sufficient professional development around the new standards. It also examines administrators' perceptions about their staff's preparedness, as well as their feelings about being able to support school staff in their work with the new standards.

Teacher Preparedness to Implement CCSS

Adoption of the CCSS brought enormous change to schools and staff in CPS. Teachers had to reconsider their instructional practices, identify new instructional materials, and help students adjust to a more demanding set of expectations about what they need to learn.

Despite these changes, around half of elementary teachers and 40 percent of high school teachers felt very familiar with the standards and very prepared to teach them in 2014. By contrast, around 10 percent of elementary teachers and 20 percent of high school teachers reported feeling not at all or only a little prepared.

Teachers in both grade levels felt far less prepared when asked if they had received sufficient curricular materials to teach the standards and sufficient professional development (**see Figure 12**). This is not altogether surprising, given the district's decision to delay purchases of curricular materials until 2015 and the limited professional development reported by many teachers (see Chapter 2).

In 2015, both elementary and high school teachers reported greater levels of familiarity with the standards and preparation to teach the standards, although the increase was more evident among elementary teachers than high school teachers. Given that 2015 was the second year of full implementation of the ELA standards and the first year of full implementation for the math standards, it's possible that as teachers spent more time teaching the new standards, they felt increasingly comfortable with them.

Elementary teachers were also more likely in 2015 than in 2014 to say they were very prepared in terms of having sufficient curricular and instructional materials and also sufficient professional development needed for teaching the standards. Yet, still only one-third felt this way in 2015. High school teachers were not much more likely to feel very prepared in terms of having sufficient curriculum materials or training in 2015 compared to 2014.

---

[27] Tschannen-Moran & Woolfolk Hoy (2001).
[28] Berman, McLaughlin, Bass, Pauly, & Zellman (1977); Guskey (1988); Stein & Wang (1988).
[29] Midgley, Feldlaufer, & Eccles (1989); Armor et al. (1976); Ashton & Webb (1986); Ross (1992).

FIGURE 12

Teachers were More Likely to Feel Very Prepared to Teach the CCSS in 2015 than 2014, with Elementary Teachers Showing Greater Increases than High School Teachers

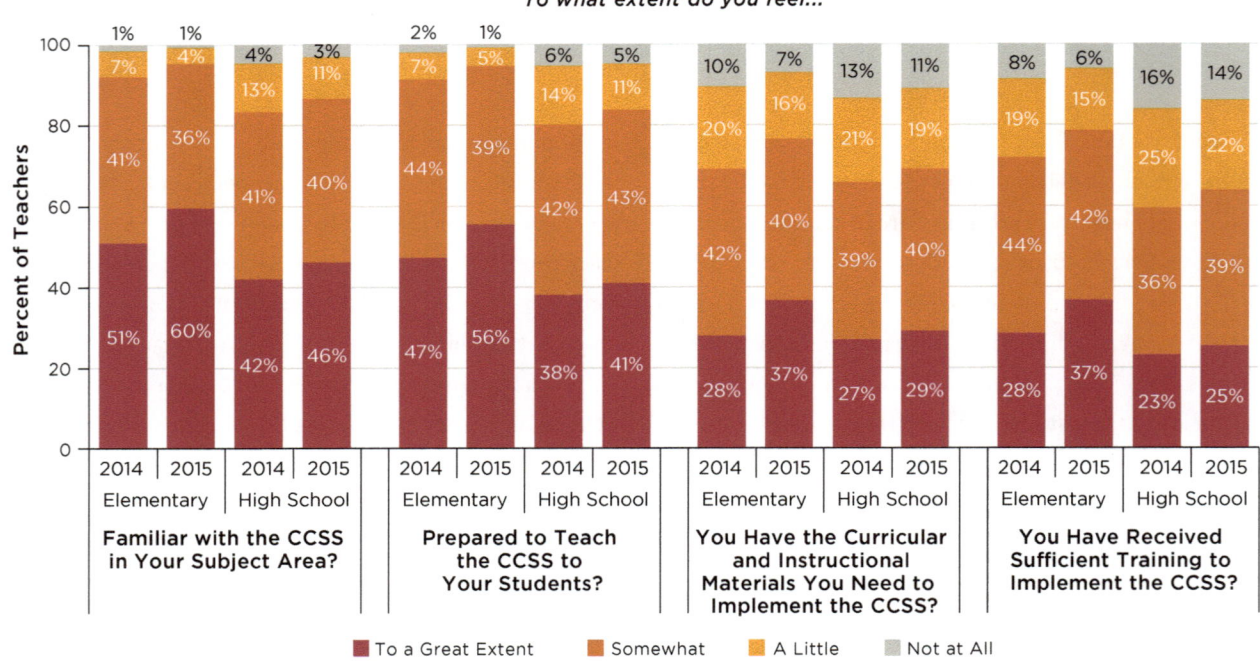

Is Professional Development Related to How Prepared Teachers Felt to Teach the Standards?

Teachers who reported more extensive professional development felt more prepared to teach the standards than teachers whose professional development experiences were not very extensive. Two-thirds of teachers who reported highly-extensive professional development felt highly prepared to teach the standards, compared to only 35 percent of teachers who had only somewhat-extensive professional development and 12 percent of teachers with not very extensive professional development (**Figure B**).

FIGURE B

Teachers with More Extensive Professional Development Were Much More Likely to Report Being Highly Prepared to Teach the CCSS than Teachers with Less Extensive Professional Development

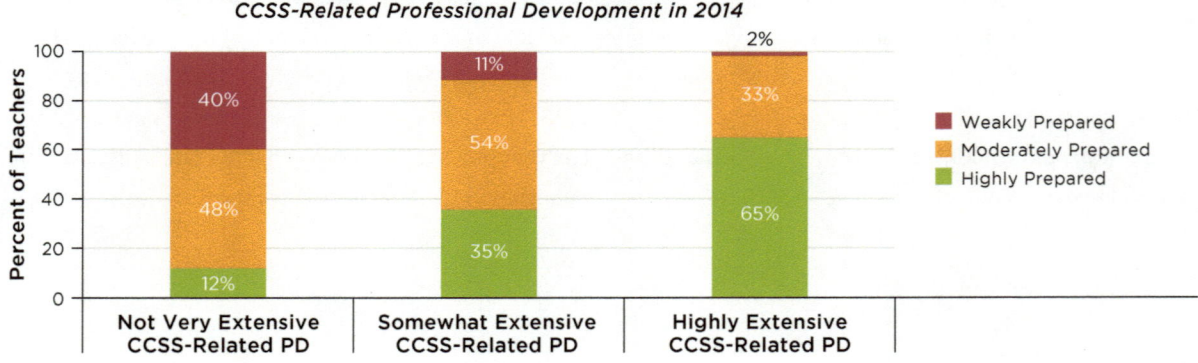

Note: Extensiveness of standards-related professional development is measured by combining the teachers' responses about the frequency of professional development they experienced with the topics covered in those session. Preparedness to teach the standards is measured by combining the four items shown in Figure 12. See Appendix A for additional details on each of these measures.

Chapter 3 | Practitioner Feelings of Preparedness to Teach the CCSS

Administrator Preparedness to Support CCSS Implementation

Administrators were much less confident than teachers in their assessment of how prepared their staff was to teach the new standards (**Figure 13**). Only a third of elementary administrators and a fifth of high school administrators said their teachers were very familiar with the new standards in their subject areas. Even fewer—21 percent of elementary administrators and 15 percent of high school administrators—felt the teachers were very prepared to teach the new standards. Only a fifth of all administrators responded their school was very prepared in terms of having the curricular materials needed to teach the new standards.

In addition to a lack of confidence about their teachers' preparation, administrators were not very confident in their own preparation to support standards implementation in 2014. Less than a quarter of all administrators felt very prepared in terms of the training they had received to implement Common Core, and less than a third felt very prepared in terms of being able to prioritize Common Core, given other pressing needs. Across both areas, high school administrators reported feeling less prepared than elementary administrators. Only 30 percent of elementary administrators, and 22 percent of high school administrators, felt very prepared to evaluate teachers on their implementation of Common Core (**Figure 14**). Given the importance of feedback and coaching for helping teachers master new skills, this may be a high priority for administrator professional development going forward.

FIGURE 13

Administrators Were Not as Confident as Teachers in Their Staff's Familiarity and Preparation to Teach the CCSS in 2014

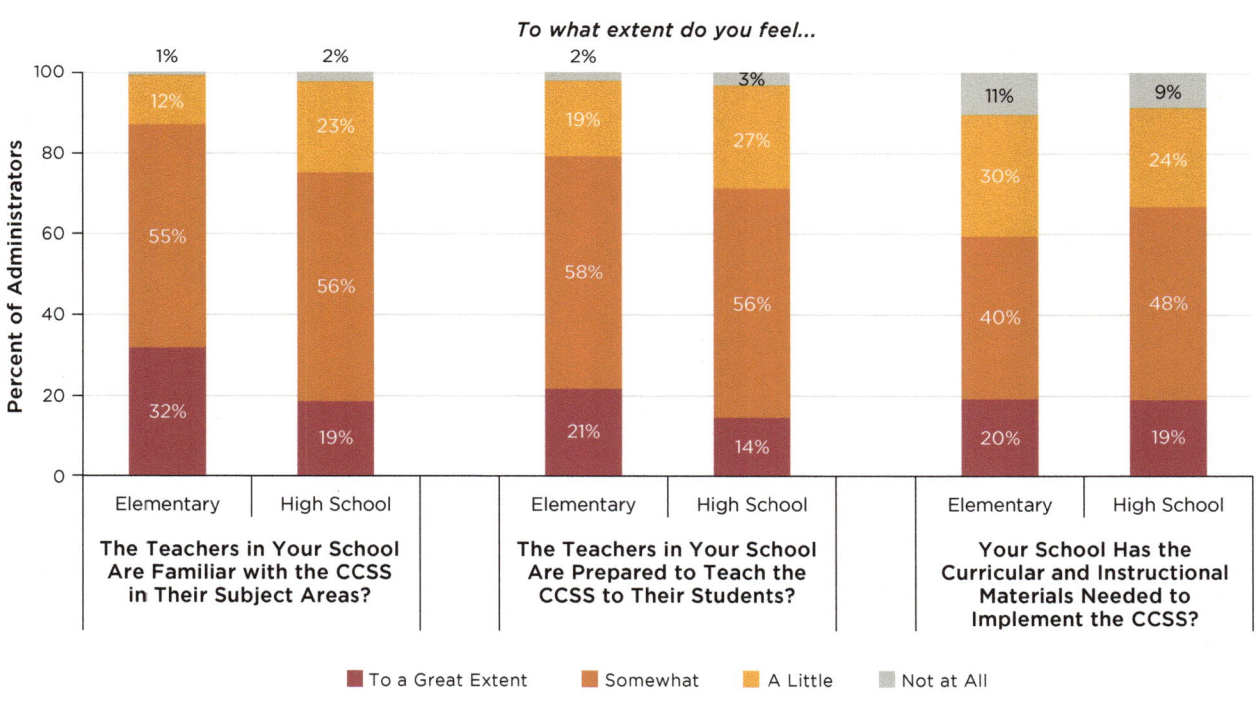

Note: These items were only included on the 2014 Administrator Survey. Percentages may not add up to 100 due to rounding.

FIGURE 14

Administrators Were Less Confident than Teachers in Their Preparation to Implement the CCSS

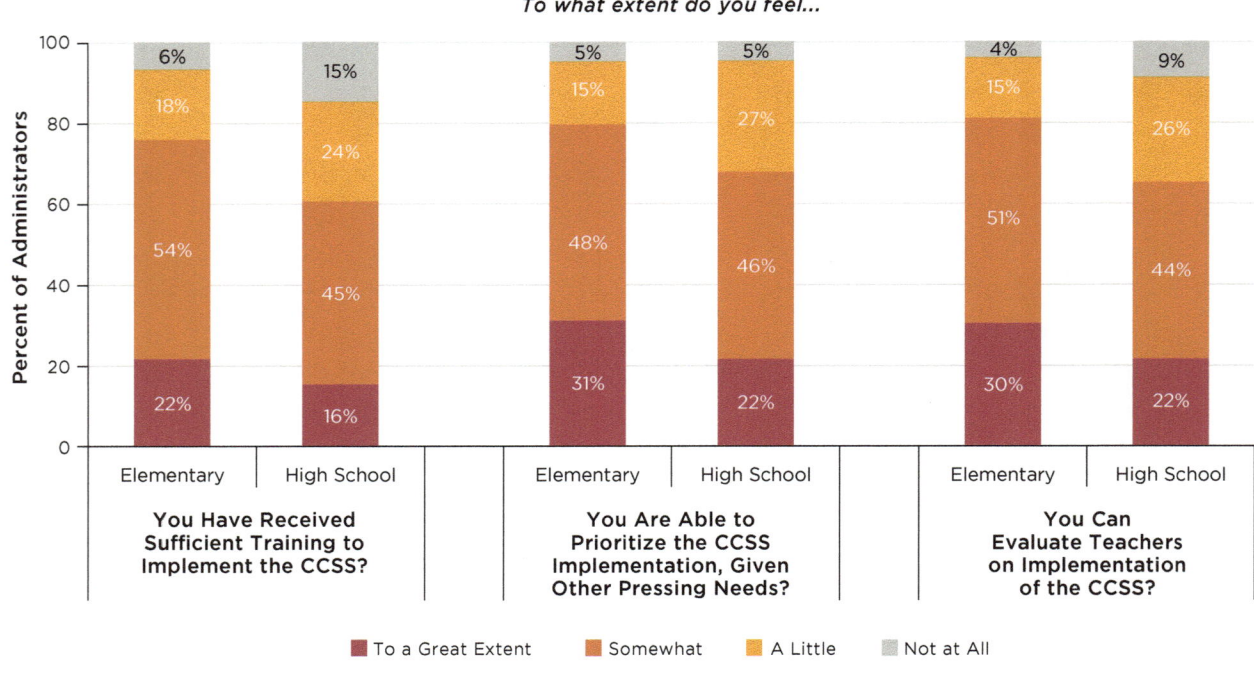

Note: These items were only included on the 2014 Administrator Survey. Percentages may not add up to 100 due to rounding.

CHAPTER 4

Schools' Organizational Capacity and Preparation for the CCSS

The district's strategy for providing CCSS-related professional development for its teachers relied heavily on schools and their staffs to ensure that teachers received the preparation they needed to implement the standards. Beginning in 2013, CPS schools sent one or two teachers to network- or district-run workshops for training around the new standards, and in turn, these teacher leaders were responsible for providing professional development to colleagues in their school. The quality and extensiveness of professional development at the school level depended in part on the skills and ability of teacher leaders to effectively impart their own knowledge and training, but it may have also depended on the schools' capacity to support these efforts. Schools which prioritized this type of professional learning and set aside time for all teachers to attend these sessions may have been more effective in preparing their teachers for the demands that came with teaching the new standards.

Instructional leadership has been identified as a critical factor in whether schools are able to improve students' learning outcomes.[30] One of the ways that strong instructional leaders promote school improvement is by prioritizing the professional capacity of their staff despite the demands of many other administrative responsibilities.[31] This may occur through very specific tasks, such as ensuring teachers have access to high-quality professional development, or through more diffuse activities, such as promoting a strong sense of collaboration and shared sense of responsibility for ensuring that all students are learning.[32] Teachers who are able to collaborate around problems of practice may be better positioned to identify instructional strategies and supports that address the needs of their students and they may be more effective in implementing policies and practices that address these needs. Strong collaboration among teachers has also been shown to be a critical factor in improving schools.[33]

As the district implemented its plan for providing professional development to teachers on the new standards, schools with high levels of instructional leadership, teacher collaboration or teacher influence may have been better positioned to ensure that this training reached their staff, given the "train-the-trainer" model. This chapter examines whether these components of schools' organizational capacity were related to teacher reports about standards-related professional development and teacher reports about how prepared they felt to teach the standards.

Organizational Capacity and Teacher Preparedness to Implement CCSS

Figure 15 shows the relationship between different components of schools' organizational capacity and teachers' reports about how extensive their standards-related professional development was. Of the components examined, instructional leadership was most strongly associated with teacher reports about standards-related professional development. Teachers who worked in schools with high levels of instructional leadership reported that their standards-related professional development was about a half a standard deviation more extensive than teachers who worked in schools with low levels of instructional leadership, a fairly sizeable difference. High levels of teacher collaboration and teacher influence were also associated with more extensive standards-related professional development, although their relationship with professional development was not as strong as instructional leadership.

---

30 Bryk et al. (2010).
31 Louis, Leithwood, Wahlstrom, & Anderson (2010); Leithwood, Louis, Anderson, & Wahlstrom (2004).
32 Louis et al. (2010); Bryk et al. (2010).
33 Bryk et al. (2010); McLaughlin & Talbert (2006); Louis, Marks, & Kruse (1996).

FIGURE 15

Schools with High Levels of Organizational Capacity Offered Significantly More Extensive CCSS-Related Professional Development than Schools with Low Levels of Organizational Capacity

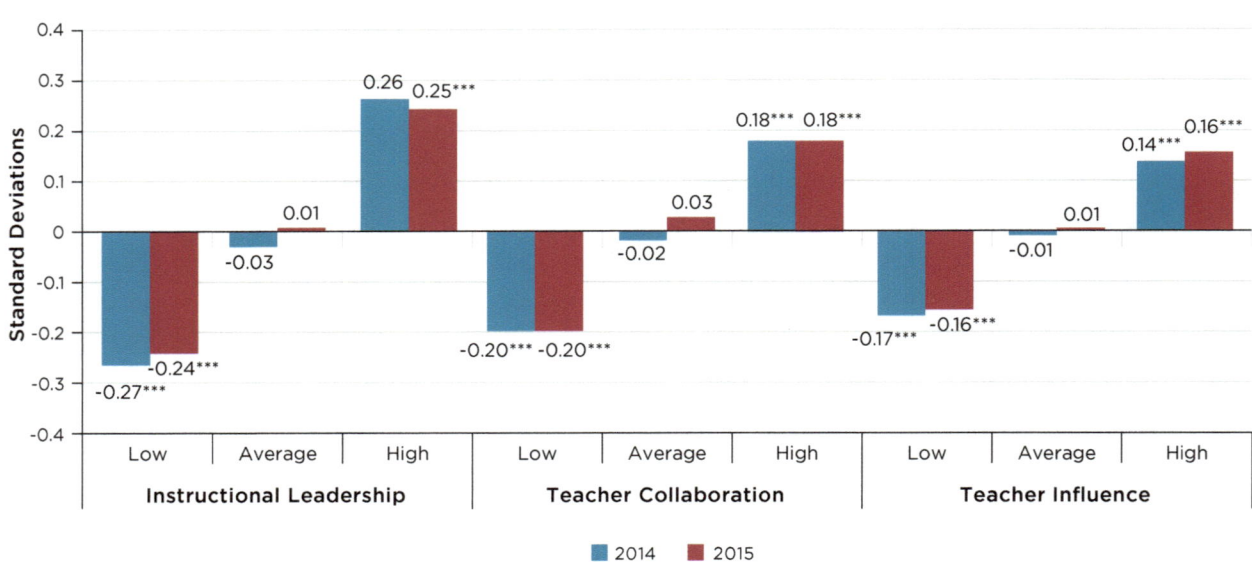

Extensiveness of CCSS-Related Professional Development in 2014 and 2015, by School Organizational Capacity

Note: Extensiveness of standards-related professional development is measured by combining teacher responses about the frequency of professional development with responses about the items covered in these sessions. This measure has been standardized so that 0 represents the district average. Measures of schools' organizational capacity also come from teacher survey responses about their school (details are provided in Appendix A). Schools are divided into three equal-sized groups for each measure of organizational capacity. The extensiveness of professional development based on schools' organizational capacity is estimated using a 2-level HLM model in which teacher responses are nested within their schools. The model also controls for the average achievement level of the school and whether it is an elementary or high school. A * indicates the teachers' responses in schools with low or high levels of organizational capacity are significantly different from teachers' responses in schools with average levels of organizational capacity at p=.05; ** indicates significant differences at p=.01 and *** indicates significant differences at p=.001.

Of course, these three dimensions of organizational capacity tend to coincide in schools. However, when we included multiple indicators of school capacity in our statistical models, we found that instructional leadership remained the strongest predictor of extensive professional development.

Teachers in schools with high levels of organizational capacity also felt more prepared to teach the CCSS **(see Figure 16)**. As the blue bars show, having high levels of instructional leadership was most strongly associated with how prepared teachers felt to teach the CCSS in 2014, but working in a school with high levels of teacher collaboration and teacher influence were also associated with teachers' feeling more prepared. In part, this is because professional development in these schools was more extensive; but even after taking this into account, organizational capacity was still significantly related to how prepared teachers felt. This suggests that there may be ways, beyond providing formal CCSS-related training, that these schools are working to prepare teachers to teach the standards.

FIGURE 16

Teachers in Schools with High Levels of Organizational Capacity Reported Feeling More Prepared to Teach the CCSS, Even After Taking into Account Their More Extensive Professional Development

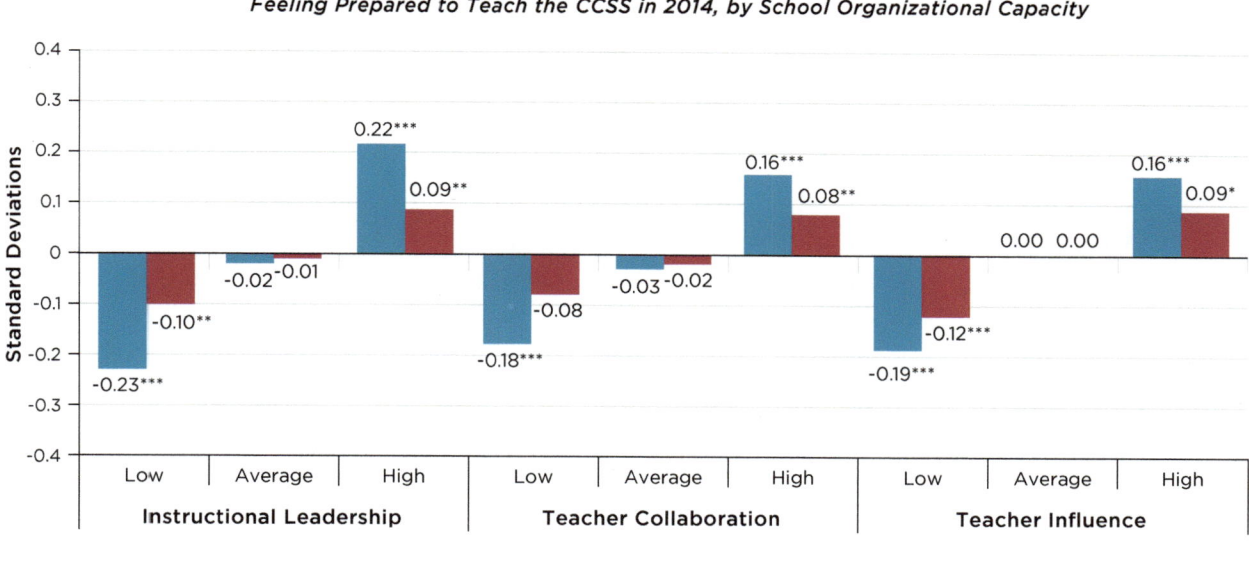

Feeling Prepared to Teach the CCSS in 2014, by School Organizational Capacity

Note: Feeling prepared to teach the standards is measured by combining teacher responses about how prepared they felt to teach the standards across several different dimensions. The measure has been standardized so that 0 represents the district average. Measures of schools' organizational capacity also come from teacher survey responses about their school (additional details are provided in Appendix A). Schools are divided into three equal-sized groups for each measure of organizational capacity. Teachers' feelings of preparedness based on schools' organizational capacity is estimated using a 2-level HLM model in which teacher responses are nested within their schools. The model also takes into account the average achievement level of the school and whether it is an elementary or high school. A * indicates the teachers' responses in schools with low or high levels of organizational capacity are significantly different from teachers' responses in schools with average levels of organizational capacity at $p=.05$; ** indicates significant differences at $p=.01$ and *** indicates significant differences at $p=.001$.

Are There Differences Across Networks in Teachers' Reports About Their CCSS-Related Professional Development and in How Prepared They Felt to Teach the Standards?

Networks also played a critical role in providing professional development to teachers around the new standards; after attending district-sponsored workshops, teacher facilitators replicated this training for teacher leaders in sessions held at their network. Moreover, some networks and their schools received additional support from university partners in preparing teachers to teach the new standards. **Figures C and D** show that teachers' reports about professional development and also their reports about how prepared they felt to teach the standards in 2014 differed considerably depending on the network to which their school belonged. During that year, schools were organized into 21 geographically-based networks. Of these, 14 were elementary school networks and five were high school networks; one was a network for charter and contract schools, and another was a network for Academy for Urban School Leadership (AUSL) schools.[D] Both the charter/contract network and the AUSL network included elementary schools and high schools, unlike the other networks which included only elementary or only high schools.

Teachers in three of the five high school networks (North-Northwest Side, South Side, and Southwest Side) reported very low levels of professional development, more than two-tenths of a standard deviation below the district average (**Figure C**). Somewhat surprisingly, only teachers in one of these high school networks,

FIGURE C

Teachers in Most High School Networks and in the Charter/Contract Network Reported Much Less Extensive CCSS-Related Professional Development in 2014 Than Teachers in Other Networks

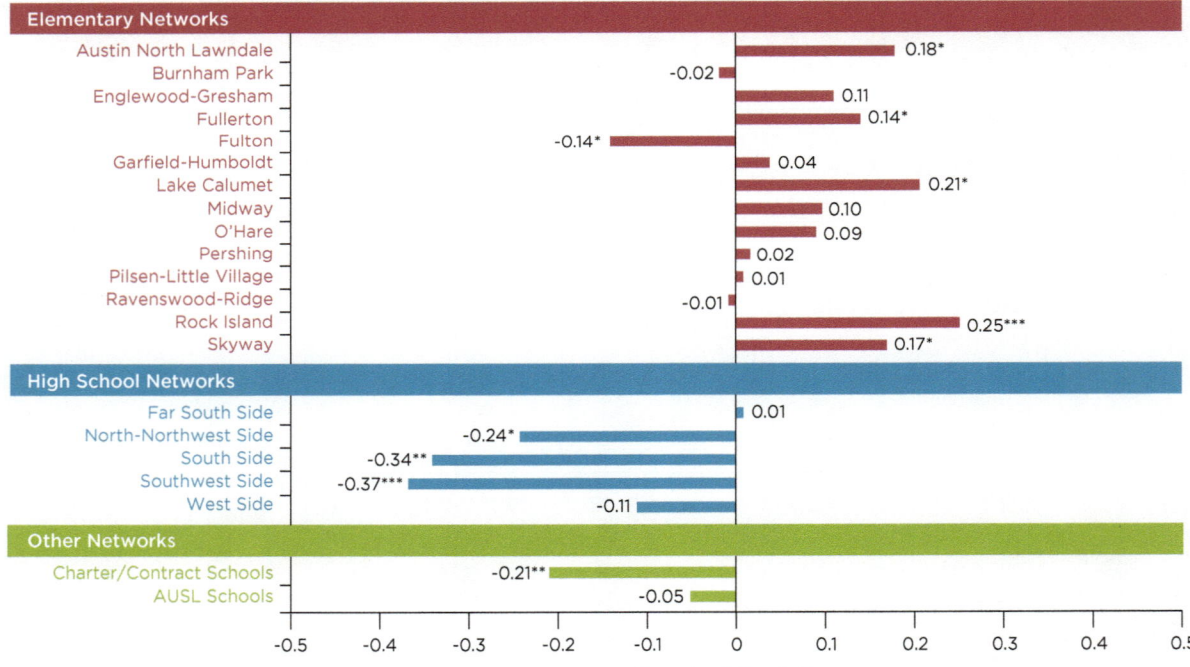

Extensiveness of CCSS-Related Professional Development in 2014, by Network

Note: The extensiveness of professional development based on schools' network affiliation is estimated using a 2-level no-intercept HLM model in which teacher responses are nested within their schools. Dummy variables are included at level 2 to indicate schools' network affiliations. The measure has been standardized so that 0 represents the district average. A * indicates that the average response of teachers' in a given network are significantly different than the district average at p=.05; ** indicates significant differences from the district average at p=.01 and *** indicates significant differences from the district average at p=.001.

D AUSL schools offer a teacher residency program for training teachers in their 31 CPS schools.

ARE THERE DIFFERENCES ACROSS NETWORKS... CONTINUED

Southwest Side Network, reported significantly lower levels of preparedness for teaching the standards (**Figure D**). Despite low levels of professional development, teachers in the other high school networks (North-Northwest, South Side, and West Side Networks) reported being more prepared than the district average, although these differences are not significant. Teachers in charter and contract schools reported similarly low levels of professional development and also low levels of preparedness to teach the standards; even once their low levels of professional development were taken into account, they reported feeling significantly less prepared to teach the standards than the district average.

Teachers in several elementary networks—including Austin-North Lawndale, Fullerton, Lake Calumet, Rock Island, and Skyway—reported significantly higher levels of professional development than the district average (**Figure C**). For teachers in most of these networks, with the exception of Lake Calumet and Skyway, their more extensive professional development was consistent with feeling more prepared to teach the standards (**Figure D**).

Networks were reorganized for the 2014-15 school year; teacher reports about their 2015 standards-related professional development still varied considerably depending on the network they were in, as did their feelings of being prepared to teach the standards. See Figures B.4 and B.5 in Appendix B.

FIGURE D

Teachers in Elementary Networks Reported Feeling More Prepared to Teach the CCSS in 2014, Largely Due to Their More Extensive Professional Development That Year

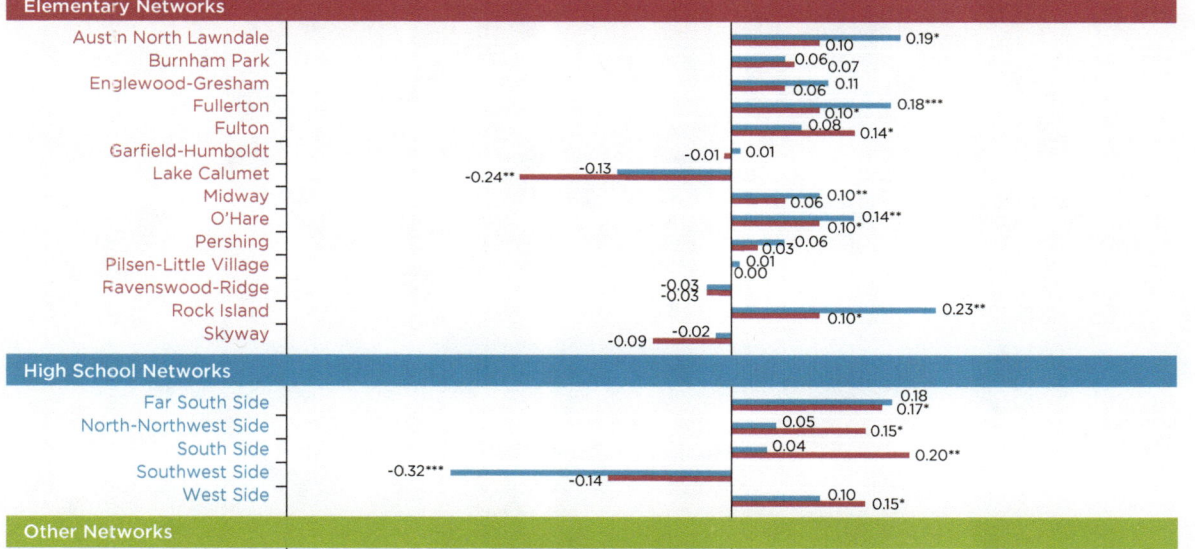

Feeling Prepared to Teach the CCSS in 2014, by Network

■ 2014 Without Taking into Account PD   ■ 2014 Taking into Account PD

Note: Teachers feelings of preparedness based on schools' network affiliation is estimated using a 2-level no-intercept HLM model in which teacher responses are nested within their schools. Dummy variables are included at level 2 to indicate each school's network affiliation. The measure has been standardized so that 0 represents the district average. A * indicates that the average responses of teachers' in a given network are significantly different than the district average at p=.05; ** indicates significant differences from the district average at p=.01 and *** indicates significant differences from the district average at p=.001.

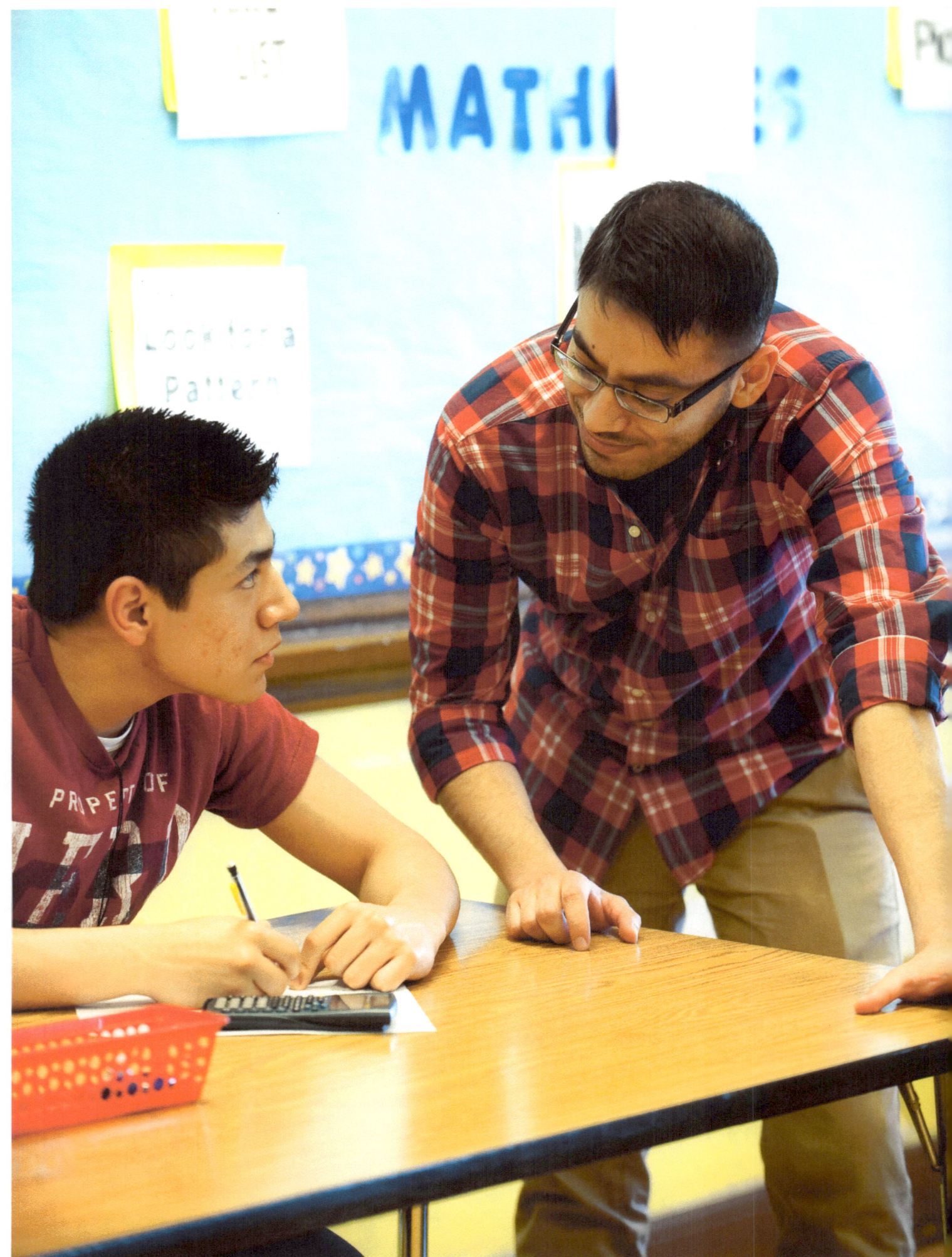

CHAPTER 5

Interpretive Summary

For over 30 years, since the publication of *A Nation at Risk*, education reform has largely focused on strengthening standards as a means of improving student achievement. Although our definition of what stronger standards entail has evolved over time—from higher graduation requirements, to more rigorous academic content, to the use of assessments to monitor student performance—the Common Core State Standards are the latest iteration of standards-based education reform.[34]

In Illinois, the new standards require a significant shift toward more rigorous content matter and skill development than what the previous standards required. This may mean that many teachers must change their instructional practices so that their teaching is more closely aligned with the goals of the CCSS. With a labor force of over 20,000 teachers in more than 600 schools, this has been no easy task for CPS.

Many CPS teachers, especially at the elementary level, were optimistic about the impact the CCSS would have on teaching and learning as implementation began. To support the implementation of the new standards, the district pursued some innovative strategies, including a multi-year commitment to providing professional development to staff and a partnership with local university staff for math training. Yet many teachers reported participating in only a few professional development sessions each year, suggesting that the impact of the new standards on teaching and learning may be uneven across the district, at least initially. Although the substantial increase in the number of teachers, particularly elementary teachers, who felt very prepared to teach the standards in 2015 compared to 2014 is a positive sign, ongoing professional learning for *all* teachers responsible for implementing the standards is likely to be critical if the goals of Common Core—improved student achievement—are to be realized.

Going forward, a more intensive focus on administrator professional development may be particularly beneficial. Research has shown that one of the most critical factors in changing teacher practice is the provision of coaching as teachers work to master new skills. The new CPS teacher evaluation system now includes 2-4 classroom observations per year for each CPS teacher, followed by a post-observation conference. While this level of feedback may be far less than what is involved in a typical coaching scenario, CPS teachers reported during the first and second years that the new teacher evaluation system was implemented that feedback from observations was constructive and helped them improve their teaching.[35] Yet, as this report has shown, administrators do not feel particularly well prepared to provide feedback to teachers specifically on how well they are implementing Common Core. Targeted support in this area may prove useful to administrators as they work to support teachers in improving their instructional practice.

More targeted support for high school teachers may also be necessary. High school teachers lag behind their elementary colleagues in the frequency

---

34 Hamilton, Stecher, & Yuan (2008).

35 Jiang, Sporte, & Luppescu (2015).

and extensiveness of their standards-related professional development and also in how prepared they feel to teach the standards. The goal of the CCSS is to ensure that students are on-track to be successful in college and in their careers. This is particularly critical during high school, as students develop the specific skills and knowledge they need for post-secondary success. But if teachers struggle with implementing the standards as they are intended, these goals are unlikely to be realized. Going forward, professional development for high school teachers may benefit from recognition of and support for the distinct challenges faced by them, particularly the fact that their current students may not have had the benefit of exposure to the new standards in earlier grades. When coursework becomes too challenging, research has shown that students can withdraw if they do not feel like they have the academic support they need.[36] The ultimate form of withdrawing from school is dropping out. Given the strides that CPS high schools and their students have made improving high school graduation rates, any reversal of this trend would be a setback.

Beyond professional development, another issue which may also play a role in how effective the new standards are in improving student outcomes is that schools are required to administer standardized tests that are not aligned to the CCSS, but are required for state or local accountability purposes. For example, elementary teachers are under a great deal of pressure to ensure their students are making sufficient gains on skills measured by the NWEA MAP tests, since low gains can negatively impact their school's accountability rating. But preparing students for these tests is likely to take away from time spent teaching the new standards, thereby diminishing the standards' potential for improving student achievement.[37]

Perhaps the most important finding of this report is that schools' organizational capacity matters quite a bit in terms of the professional development teachers received and how prepared they felt to teach the new standards. Additional research is needed to understand exactly what schools with high levels of instructional leadership, teacher collaboration, and teacher influence have done to support the implementation of Common Core. Nevertheless, the findings in this report suggest that they have found ways to supplement the district plan so that their teachers have far more opportunities for professional learning on the new standards and as a result feel more prepared to teach them. Whether this means relying on their own staff for ongoing professional development or leveraging external partnerships for additional support is not clear. Nevertheless, this finding serves as a reminder that investing in schools' organizational capacity, particularly by developing strong instructional leadership, is not only critical for the successful implementation of the Common Core State Standards but also for the success of school improvement more broadly.

---

36 Allensworth et al. (2014).
37 The Illinois State Board of Education recently announced that it will no longer require high school students to take the PARCC exam and will instead administer the SAT for free, elementary schools are still required to administer NWEA Map tests as a part of the district's accountability system (Rado, 2016).

References

Achieve, The Education Trust, & Thomas B. Fordham Foundation. (2004)
The American Diploma Project: Ready or not: Creating a high school diploma that counts. Washington, DC: Achieve, Inc.

ACT, Inc. (2012)
The condition of college & career readiness. Iowa City, IA: ACT.

Allensworth, E.M., Gwynne, J.A., Pareja, A.S., Sebastian, J., & Stevens, W.D. (2014)
Setting the stage for academic challenge: Classroom control and student support. Chicago, IL: University of Chicago Consortium on Chicago School Research.

Armor, D., Conroy-Oseguera, P., Cox, M., King, N., McDonnell, L., Pascal, A., Pauly, E., & Zellman, G. (1976)
Analysis of the school preferred reading programs in selected Los Angeles minority schools (Report R-2007-LAUSD). Santa Monica, CA: Rand Corporation.

Ashton, P.T., & Webb, R.B. (1986)
Making a difference: Teachers' sense of efficacy and student achievement. New York, NY: Longman.

Berman, P., McLaughlin, M., Bass, G., Pauly, E., & Zellman, G. (1977)
Federal programs supporting educational change. Vol. VII: Factors affecting implementation and continuation (Report R-1589/7-HEW). Santa Monica, CA: The Rand Corporation.

Bryk, A., Sebring, P.B., Allensworth, E., Luppescu S., & Easton, J.Q. (2010)
Organizing schools for improvement: Lessons from Chicago. Chicago, IL: University of Chicago Press.

Carmichael, S.B., Martino, G., Porter-Magee, K., & Wilson, W.S. (2010)
The state of state standards—and the Common Core—in 2010. Washington, DC: Thomas B. Fordham Foundation.

Chicago Public Schools. (2015)
Chicago Public Schools: State of Literacy. Retrieved from http://chicagoliteracyalliance.org/wp-content/uploads/2015/12/CLA-STATE.pptxES-1.pdf

Chicago Public Schools. (n.d.)
Common Core English Language Arts/Literacy PD at CPS. Chicago, IL: Chicago Public Schools.

Coburn, C., Hill, H., & Spillane, J. (2016)
Alignment and accountability in policy design and implementation: The Common Core State Standards and implementation research. *Educational Researcher, 45*(4), 243-251.

Common Core Standards Initiative. (2014)
Frequently asked questions. Retrieved from http://www.corestandards.org/about-the-standards/

Conley, D. (2014)
The Common Core State Standards: Insight into their development and purpose. Washington, DC: Council of Chief State School Officers.

Darling-Hammond, L., Chung Wei, R., Andree, A., & Richardson, N. (2009)
Professional learning in the learning profession: A status report on teacher development in the United States and abroad. Oxford, OH: National Staff Development Council.

Datnow, A., & Castellano, M. (2000)
Teachers' responses to Success for All: How beliefs, experiences and adaptations shape implementation. *American Educational Research Journal, 37*(3), 775-799.

Dembo, M., & Gibson, S. (1985)
Teachers sense of efficacy: An important factor in school improvement. *The Elementary School Journal, 86*(2), 173-184.

Donnell, L.A., & Gettinger, M. (2015)
Elementary school teachers acceptability of school reform: Contribution of belief congruence, self-efficacy and professional development. *Teaching and Teacher Education, 51*, 47-57.

French, V.W. (1997)
Teachers must be learners, too: Professional development and national teaching standards. *NASSP Bulletin, 81*(585), 38-44.

Gold, B. (2002)
Social construction of urban education: New Jersey whole school reform and teachers' understanding of social class and race. New York, NY: Pace University.

Gulamhussein, A. (2013)
The core of professional development. *American School Board Journal, 2013,* 36-37.

Guskey, T.R. (1988)
Teacher efficacy, self-concept, and attitudes toward the implementation of instructional innovation. *Teaching and Teacher Education, 4*(1), 63-69.

Hamilton, L., Stecher, B., & Yuan, K. (2008)
Standards-based reform in the United States: History, research and future directions. Washington, DC: The Rand Corporation.

Hargreaves, A. (2005)
Educational change takes ages: Life, career and generational factors in teachers' emotional responses to educational change. *Teaching and Teacher Education, 21*(8), 967-983.

Honig, M. (2006)
Complexity and policy implementation: Challenges and opportunities for the field. In M. Honig (Ed.), *New directions in education policy implementation* (pp. 1-24). Albany, NY: State University of New York.

Jiang, J., Sporte, S.E., & Luppescu, S. (2015)
Teacher perspectives on evaluation reform: Chicago's REACH Students. *Educational Researcher, 44*(2), 105-116.

Kane, T.J., Owens, A.M., Marinell, W.H., Thal, D.R.C., Staiger, D.O. (2016)
Teaching higher: Educators' perspectives on Common Core implementation. Boston, MA: Harvard University, Center for Education Policy Research.

Louis, K.S., & Dentler, R. (1988)
Knowledge use and school improvement. *Curriculum Inquiry, 18*(1), 32-62.

Louis, K.S., Febey, K., & Shroeder, R. (2005)
State-mandated accountability in high schools: Teachers' interpretations of a new era. *Educational Evaluation and Policy Analysis, 27*(2), 177-204.

Louis, K.S., Leithwood, K., Wahlstrom, K., & Anderson, S. (2010)
Learning from leadership: Investigating the links to improved student learning. Minneapolis, MN: University of Minnesota.

Louis, K.S., Marks, H., & Kruse, S. (1996)
Teachers' professional community in restructuring schools. *American Educational Research Journal, 33*(4), 757-98.

Leithwood, K., Louis, K.S., Anderson, S., & Wahlstrom, K. (2004)
How leadership influences student learning. Minneapolis, MN: University of Minnesota.

McLaughlin, M., & Talbert, J. (2006)
Building school-based teacher learning communities: Professional strategies to improve student achievement. New York, NY: Teachers College Press.

Mumtaz, S. (2000)
Factors affecting teachers' use of information and communications technology: A review of the literature. *Journal of Information Technology for Teacher Education, 9*(3), 319-341.

Midgley, C., Feldlaufer, H., & Eccles, J. (1989)
Change in teacher efficacy and student self- and task-related beliefs in mathematics during the transition to junior high school. *Journal of Educational Psychology, 81*(2), 247-258.

National Academy of Education. (2009)
Standards, assessments, and accountability: Education policy white paper. Washington, DC: National Academy of Education.

Rado, D. (2016, July 12)
Illinois ends much-debated PARCC test for high school students. *Chicago Tribune.* Retrieved from http://www.chicagotribune.com/news/local/breaking/ct-parcc-test-high-school-met-20160711-story.html

Ross, J.A. (1992)
Teacher efficacy and the effect of coaching on student achievement. *Canadian Journal of Education, 17*(1), 51-65.

Stein, M.K., & Wang, M.C. (1988)
Teacher development and school improvement: The process of teacher change. *Teaching and Teacher Education, 4*(2), 171-187.

Truesdale, W.T. (2003)
The implementation of peer coaching on the transferability of staff development to classroom practice in two selected Chicago public elementary schools. *Dissertation Abstracts International, 64*(11), 3923.

Tschannen-Moran, M., & Woolfolk Hoy, A. (2001)
Teacher efficacy: Capturing an elusive construct. *Teaching and Teacher Education, 17*(7), 783-805.

Witt, J.C., & Elliott, S.N. (1985)
Acceptability of classroom intervention strategies. In T.R. Kratochwill (Ed.), *Advances in school psychology* (4) (pp. 251-288). London, UK: Routledge.

Appendix A
Data and Methods

Sample

This report uses survey responses to examine CPS teachers' and administrators' experiences with the CCSS. Each year, the UChicago Consortium administers a districtwide survey, *My Voice, My School*, to all teachers in CPS. In 2014 and 2015, the annual teacher survey included a series of questions about the CCSS, which were asked of teachers who either taught in self-contained classrooms or were subject-specific teachers. Among respondents who indicated that they taught a specific subject, only those whose primary subject was ELA or math were included in the analyses. In 2014, there were 10,147 self-contained or subject specific teachers who taught in 609 regular CPS schools and who completed the survey; in 2015 there were 10,304 self-contained or subject specific teachers in 612 regular CPS schools who completed the survey. The overall response rates for the teacher surveys in these two years were 80.9 percent in 2014 and 80.7 percent in 2015; these rates include all teachers, not just those who were subject-specific or self-contained. In 2014 and 2015, the UChicago Consortium also administered surveys to principals and assistant principals. The response rates for these surveys were 59.8 percent in 2014 and 42.2 percent in 2015.

Statistical Tests of Differences Between Elementary and High School Practitioners' Responses on Survey Items

We tested whether elementary and high school practitioners' responses on survey items were significantly different using a chi-square statistic. We found that elementary and high school teachers had statistically different responses on each survey item included in this report. Elementary and high school administrators also had statistically different responses on many items, but not all. **Table A.1** provides a list of the seven survey items for which the responses of elementary and high school administrators were not statistically different; it

TABLE A.1

Survey Items for Which There Were No Statistical Differences in Responses Between Elementary and High School Administrators

Figure	Survey Item	Chi-Square Statistic and p-value
Fig 10	Which of the following steps have you taken to implement the Common Core created Leadership plan for the CCSS?	2.78 $p= 0.0986$
Fig 10	Which of the following steps have you taken to implement the Common Core modified ELA curriculum to align with the CCSS?	1.39 $p= 0.2388$
Fig 11	To what extent is each of these a barrier to implementing the CCSS in your school—inadequate PD for teachers to implement the CCSS?	4.28 $p= 0.2325$
Fig 11	To what extent is each of these a barrier to implementing the CCSS in your school—being held accountable for students assessments not aligned with the CCSS?	5.49 $p= 0.1394$
Fig 13	To what extent do you feel the teachers in your school are prepared to teach the CCSS to their students?	6.27 $p= 0.0988$
Fig 13	To what extent do you feel your school has the curricular and instructional materials needed to implement the CCSS?	3.2247 $p= 0.3583$
Fig B.2	How challenging do you think the CCSS are for students in your school?	1.47 $p= 0.6897$

also includes the chi-square statistic and corresponding p-value showing no statistical difference.

Survey Measures

We used Rasch analysis to combine teachers' responses on different items into a measure capturing a single construct. **Table A.2** provides details on the reliability of each measure used in this report and also the items that were included in each measure.

Methods

Figures in Chapters 1, 2, and 3 rely on descriptive statistics to describe teachers' and administrators' experiences with the CCSS. In Chapter 4, we examine the relationship between schools' organizational capacity and teachers' reports about how extensive their standards-related professional development was and also how prepared they felt to teach the standards. We use a 2-level hierarchical linear model (HLM) to examine these relationships. Level 1 is teacher reports about either their experiences with professional development or how prepared they felt to teach the standards. These outcomes have been standardized so that 0 represents the district average. At level 2, we use two dummy variables to indicate whether schools are above or below average on a given indicator of organizational capacity (i.e., instructional leadership, teacher collaboration, teacher influence). We also control for the achievement level of the school and for whether the school is a high school. As an example, the model examining the relationship between instructional leadership and teacher reports about extensiveness of their standards-related professional development is as follows:

$$Y_{ij} = \beta_{0j} + e_{ij}$$
$$\beta_{0j} = \gamma_{00} + \gamma_{01}(\text{Above Average Instructional Leadership})_j + \gamma_{02}(\text{Below Average Instructional Leadership})_j + \gamma_{03}(\text{High School})_j + \gamma_{04}(\text{Average Achievement})_j + u_{0j}$$

TABLE A.2
Survey Measures, Reliability, and Items

Common Core Survey Measures	Survey Items
Extensiveness of Standards-Related Professional Development Reliability=0.76	How often did you receive formal training or professional development on the CCSS this past year? Which of the following topics have been addressed in your CCSS training and professional development? • Common Core Standards in English/Language Arts and Literacy • Common Core Standards in Mathematics • Curriculum materials and resources to teach the common standards • Teaching the common standards to specific student groups (for example, students with disabilities or English language learners) • Adapting classroom assessments to the common standards • New standardized assessments aligned with the CCSS • Research on the best practices for implementation of the common standards
Feeling Prepared to Teach the Standards Reliability = 0.85	To what extent do you feel: • Familiar with the CCSS in your subject area? • Prepared to teach the CCSS to your students? • You have the curricular and instructional materials you need to implement the CCSS? • You have received sufficient training to implement the CCSS? • [HS Teachers only] The CCSS is integrated into the instructional practices of teachers in your department? • [HS Teachers only] The CCSS is integrated into the instructional practices of teachers in your school?

Organizational Capacity Measures	Survey Items
Instructional Leadership Reliability = 0.90	The principal at this school: • Makes clear to the staff his or her expectations for meeting instructional goals. • Communicates a clear vision for our school. • Understands how children learn. • Sets high standards for student learning. • Presses teachers to implement what they have learned in professional development. • Carefully tracks student academic progress. • Knows what's going on in my classroom. • Participates in instructional planning with teams of teachers.
Teacher Collaboration Reliability = 0.69	This school year, how often have you: • Observed another teacher's classroom to offer feedback? • Observed another teacher's classroom to get ideas for your own instruction? • Gone over student assessment data with other teachers to make instructional decisions? • Worked with other teachers to develop materials or activities for particular classes? • Worked on instructional strategies with other teachers?
Teacher Influence Reliability = 0.76	How much influence do teachers have over school policy in each of the areas below? • Planning how discretionary school funds should be used. • Determining books and other instructional materials used in classrooms. • Establishing the curriculum and instructional program. • Determining the content of in-service programs. • Setting the standards for student behavior.

Appendix B
Supplemental Graphs

The Impact and Challenge of CCSS

Administrators' attitudes about the impact the standards will have generally mirror those of teachers. Elementary administrators were much more likely than high school administrators to say that the new standards will have a great deal of impact on teaching and student achievement. Both groups felt the standards would have less impact on student achievement than on teaching, but elementary administrators were more likely to say the standards would have a great deal of impact on student achievement than their high school colleagues (**Figure B.1**). Like teachers, most administrators feel the new standards are very challenging for the students in their school (**Figure B.2**).

Most Helpful Sources of CCSS-Related Professional Development

Administrators were asked to identify which sources of professional development were most helpful for training on the new math and ELA standards. Elementary administrators were most likely to say that professional development provided by the networks was the most helpful source for both standards, while high school administrators were most likely to say professional development provided by their school staff was the most helpful (**Figure B.3**).

FIGURE B.1

Elementary Administrators are More Likely than High School Administrators to Say That the CCSS Will Have a Great Deal of Impact on Teaching and Learning

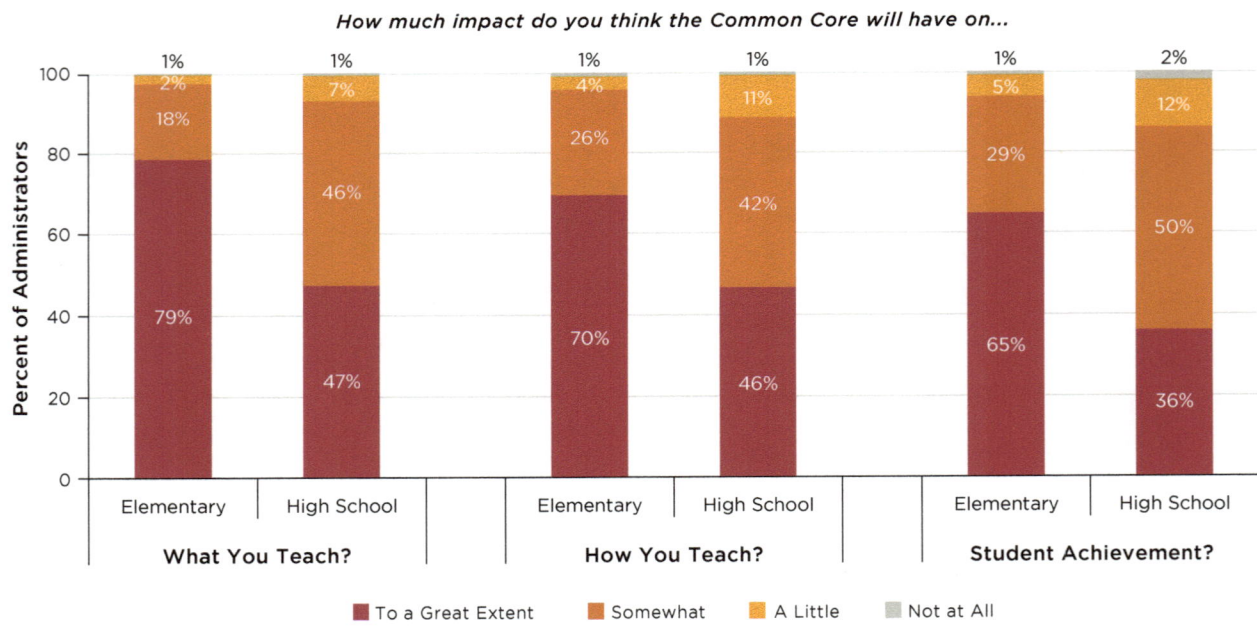

Note: These items were only included on the 2014 Administrator Survey. Percentages may not add up to 100 due to rounding.

FIGURE B.2
More Than Half of All Administrators Felt the New Standards Would be Very Challenging for the Students in their School

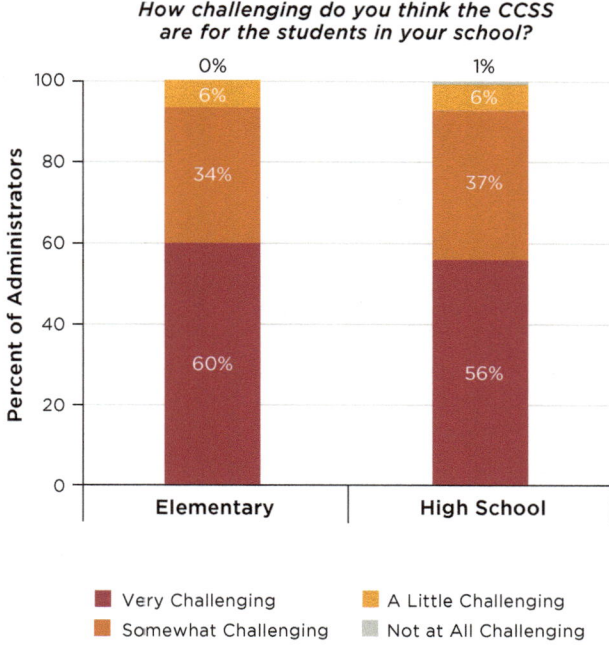

FIGURE B.3
Elementary Administrators Are More Likely to Say Network-Driven Sources of Professional Development are Most Helpful; High School Administrators Point to School-Driven Sources

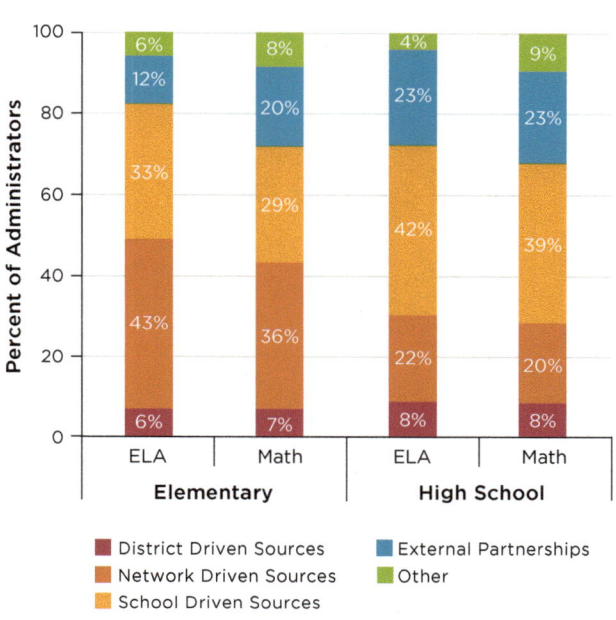

Note: This item comes from the 2014 Administrator Survey.

Note: This item comes from the 2015 Administrator Survey. Percentages may not add up to 100 due to rounding.

Differences Across Networks in 2015 CCSS-Related Professional Development and Feelings of Being Prepared to Teach the Standards

In 2015, schools were reorganized into 18 different networks, which are still in use today: Networks 1-13, the AUSL Network, the Charter Network, the Contract Schools Network, the OS4 Network, and the Service Leadership Academies. Nearly all of these networks now include both high school and elementary schools, with the exception of the Service Leadership Academies, all of which are high schools with a military focus. As shown in **Figure B.4**, teachers continued to report a wide range of experiences in the extensiveness of standards-related professional development in 2015, depending on which network their school belonged to. Teachers in charter schools reported significantly less extensive professional development than the district average, as did teachers in Network 6. Charter teachers also reported feeling less prepared to teach the standards, and this was partially due to their less-extensive professional development (**Figure B.5**). But even after taking that into account, they still felt significantly less prepared to teach the standards than the district average.

Teachers in Networks 5 and 12 reported significantly more extensive professional development than the district average (**Figure B.4**). They also reported feeling more prepared to teach the standards. Once we take into account their more-extensive professional development, teachers in Network 5 still felt significantly more prepared than the typical teacher in the district, while teachers in Network 12 were no different from the district average. While teachers in the AUSL network also reported more extensive professional development, they did not report feeling more prepared to teach the standards.

FIGURE B.4

Teachers in Networks 5 and 12 and the AUSL Network Reported Significantly More Extensive Professional Development in 2015

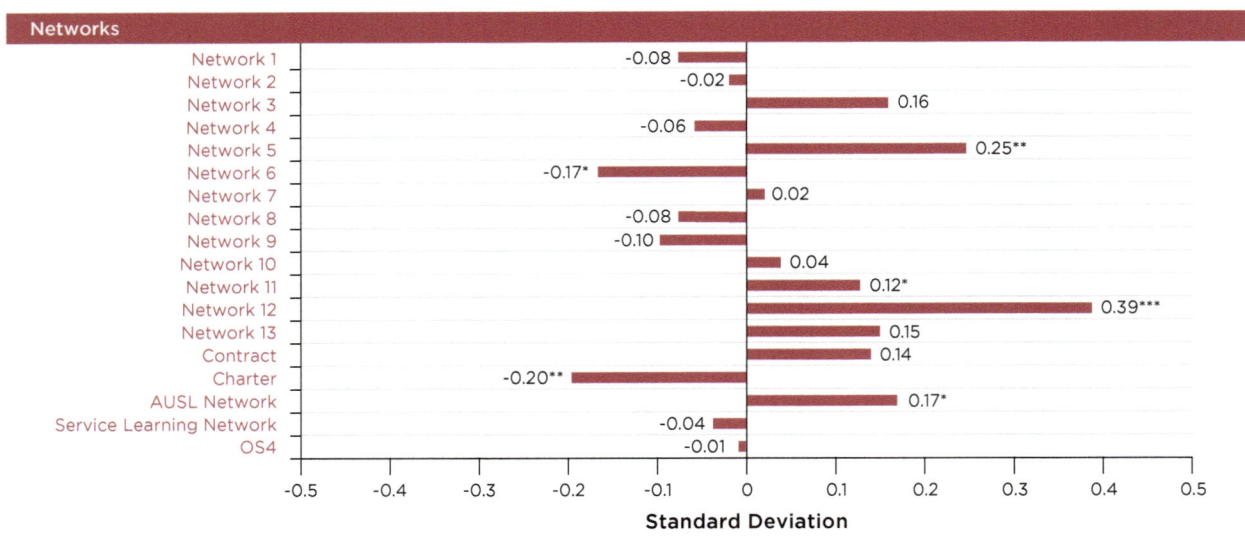

Extensiveness of CCSS-Related Professional Development in 2015, by Network

Note: The extensiveness of professional developments based on schools' network affiliation is estimated using a 2-level no-intercept HLM model in which teacher responses are nested within their schools. Dummy variables are included at level 2 to indicate each school's network affiliation. The measure has been standardized so that 0 represents the district average. A * indicates that the average response of teachers' in a given network are significantly different than the district average at p=.05; ** indicates significant differences from the district average at p=.01 and *** indicates significant differences from the district average at p=.001.

FIGURE B.5

Teachers in Network 5 and 12 Reported Feeling More Prepared to Teach the Standards, but for Network 5 This Was Only Partially Related to Their Reports of More Extensive Professional Development

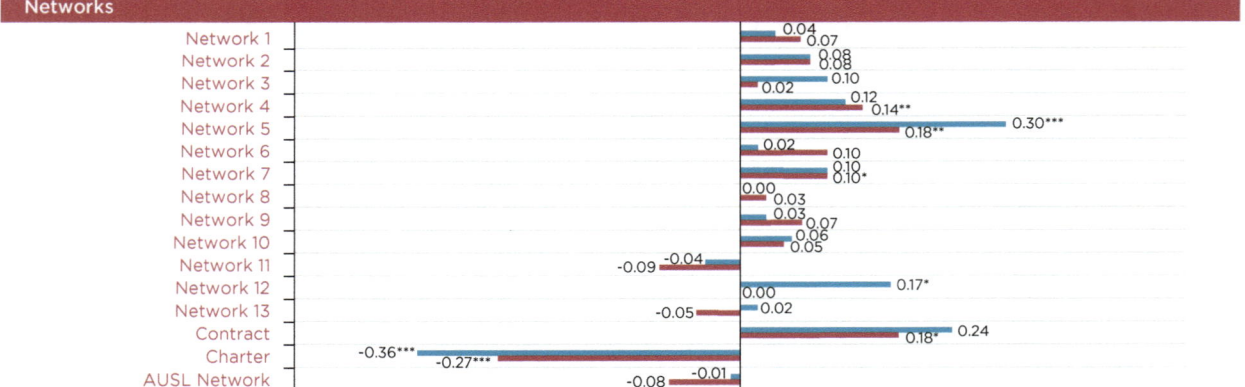

Feeling Prepared to Teach the CCSS in 2015, by Network

■ 2015 Without Taking into Account PD   ■ 2015 Taking into Account PD

Note: Teachers feelings of preparedness based on schools' network affiliation is estimated using a 2-level no-intercept HLM model in which teacher responses are nested within their schools. Dummy variables are included at level 2 to indicate each school's network affiliation. The measure has been standardized so that 0 represents the district average. A * indicates that the average responses of teachers' in a given network are significantly different than the district average at p=.05; ** indicates significant differences from the district average at p=.01 and *** indicates significant differences from the district average at p=.001.

ABOUT THE AUTHORS

JULIA A. GWYNNE is a managing director and senior research scientist at the University of Chicago Consortium on School Research. Her current work is focused on how schools are implementing new science and math standards and whether these standards have an impact on teaching and learning. She is also conducting research on charter high schools in CPS to understand whether students who attend these schools have different learning outcomes than similar students who attend non-charter high schools. Gwynne received her PhD in sociology from the University of Chicago.

JENNIFER R. COWHY is a research analyst at the University of Chicago Consortium on School Research. Her current work involves understanding the implementation of select programs and policies, including the Common Core State Standards, school closings, and a middle grades intervention. In addition, she has conducted work on teacher evaluation and teacher preparation. Cowhy received her MPP and MA in social service administration at the University of Chicago and her BA in sociology from the University of Michigan.

This report reflects the interpretation of the authors. Although the UChicago Consortium's Steering Committee provided technical advice, no formal endorsement by these individuals, organizations, or the full Consortium should be assumed.

UCHICAGO Consortium
ON SCHOOL RESEARCH

Directors

ELAINE M. ALLENSWORTH
Lewis-Sebring Director

STACY B. EHRLICH
Managing Director

JULIA A. GWYNNE
Managing Director

HOLLY HART
Survey Director

KYLIE KLEIN
Director of Research Operations

BRONWYN MCDANIEL
Director of Outreach and Communication

JENNY NAGAOKA
Deputy Director

MELISSA RODERICK
*Senior Director
Hermon Dunlap Smith Professor
School of Social Service Administration*

PENNY BENDER SEBRING
Co-Founder

MARISA DE LA TORRE
Director for Internal Research Capacity

Steering Committee

DENNIS LACEWELL
Co-Chair
Urban Prep Academy for Young Men

BRIAN SPITTLE
Co-Chair
DePaul University

Ex-Officio Members

SARA RAY STOELINGA
Urban Education Institute

Institutional Members

SARAH DICKSON
Chicago Public Schools

ELIZABETH KIRBY
Chicago Public Schools

TROY LARAVIERE
Chicago Principals and Administrators Association

KAREN G.J. LEWIS
Chicago Teachers Union

ALAN MATHER
Chicago Public Schools

TONY SMITH
Illinois State Board of Education

Individual Members

GENA CANEVA
Lindblom Math & Science Academy

CATHERINE DEUTSCH
Illinois Network of Charter Schools

RAQUEL FARMER-HINTON
University of Wisconsin, Milwaukee

KATIE HILL
Office of the Cook County State's Attorney

MEGAN HOUGARD
Chicago Public Schools

KIRABO JACKSON
Northwestern University

GREG JONES
Kenwood Academy

PRANAV KOTHARI
Revolution Impact, LLC

LILA LEFF
Umoja Student Development Corporation & Emerson Collective

RITO MARTINEZ
Surge Institute

LUISIANA MELÉNDEZ
Erikson Institute

SHAZIA MILLER
American Institutes for Research

CRISTINA PACIONE-ZAYAS
Erikson Institute

BEATRIZ PONCE DE LEÓN
Generation All

PAIGE PONDER
One Million Degrees

KATHLEEN ST. LOUIS CALIENTO
Spark Program

AMY TREADWELL
Chicago New Teacher Center

REBECCA VONDERLACK-NAVARRO
Latino Policy Forum

JOHN ZEIGLER
DePaul University